Guide to the
History of
Psychology

Guide to the History of Psychology

by

JOHN D. LAWRY
Professor of Psychology
Marymount College
Tarrytown, New York

1981

LITTLEFIELD, ADAMS & CO.

Copyright 1981 by

LITTLEFIELD, ADAMS & CO.
81 Adams Drive, Totowa, New Jersey 07512

Library of Congress Cataloging in Publication Data

Lawry, John D.
  Guide to the history of psychology.

  Bibliography: p.
  Includes indexes.
  1. Psychology—History.   2. Psychology—Philosophy—History.
I. Title.
BF81.L38   150'.9   81-13720
ISBN 0-8226-0361-6   AACR2

Printed in the United States of America

For Lili, my daughter

Contents

Preface

The idea for this book came from a unique combination of circumstances. While on sabbatical leave from Marymount College in 1978–1979, I taught as a visiting lecturer in the Far East Division of the University College of the University of Maryland. During one of the terms I was stationed in Japan, where I taught the introductory course in psychology as well as a course in the history of psychology. At the end of the term, one of my students in the introductory course indicated that he had enjoyed the course but expressed the wish that he had taken the course in the history of psychology first. When I explained that the history course is much more advanced than the introductory course, he replied that he felt a real need for some historical background throughout the introductory course. His remarks underlined for me the serious handicaps, of both a historical and philosophical nature, experienced by most undergraduates today.

The aim of this *Guide* is to provide a practical reference for individuals studying psychology who would benefit from a background in the history of ideas in the West, particularly students enrolled in the introductory course. This *Guide* may also be used as a reference for upper-level and graduate courses, especially those in which the history of psychology plays an important part. The *Guide* does not try to duplicate the many fine textbooks already available in the history of psychology but maintains an outline format and is written on a level appropriate for the beginning student of psychology. It is hoped that the *Guide* will serve as a brief introduction to the history of psychology for the lay reader as well.

The *Guide* is divided into five sections. The first section,

titled "Innovators," provides brief sketches of 118 major contributors to the historical development of psychology, from
the early Greek philosophers to such early twentieth century
figures as James, Freud, and Pavlov. The criteria that were
used to determine whether an individual would be included in
the *Guide* were: (1) frequency of appearance in the standard
histories of psychology (cf. Section V, Part I), and (2)
whether the individual's major contribution was made before
1930.

The second section, titled "Innovations," presents a com-
pilation of significant "firsts" in the history of early scientific
psychology. The section puts into perspective the topics and
issues generally included in the contemporary textbooks of
psychology by providing the usually neglected, inauspicious,
yet courageous beginnings of scientific psychology in the
eighteenth and nineteenth centuries.

The third section provides a glossary of important
philosophical terms, the meanings of which constitute the
legitimate patrimony of scientific psychology. The glossary
also contains extended discussion on the major body-mind
theories and on such important issues as the difference between psychology as a science and as philosophy.

The fourth section contains an annotated list of 115
"classics" in the history of psychology, and the fifth section
contains an annotated guide to the secondary works in the
field for those who want to study further.

It is hoped that this *Guide* will lighten the burden that too
many students experience when they encounter psychology in
the classroom for the first time. As Ebbinghaus declared
almost a hundred years ago, "Psychology has a long past but
a short history." It is the purpose of this book to illuminate
that "past" as well as to delineate the "history." Any suggestions for its improvement in future editions will be greatly ap-
preciated.

Finally, I want to thank Dr. Gladys Walterhouse, who
possesses the rare combination of editorial expertise and
philosophical training, for her patient reading of the

manuscript, her numerous suggestions for its improvement, and her kind words of encouragement.

J.D.L.
September 1981

Section I
Innovators

This section focuses on the great names in the history of psychology presented in chronological order (with a few exceptions where intellectual lineage overrides chronology) and organized according to the convention of historical periods, except for the last two chapters which tell the separate stories of experimental and clinical psychology, respectively. The format consists of enumerating the major contributions of each innovator in outline. As the title suggests, the emphasis is on originality and innovation.

Chapter 1, Classical Antiquity (600 B.C.–1000 A.D.), presents the earliest psychologists disguised in the robes of philosophy, beginning with the sixth century B.C., the moment when historians agree that philosophy was born. There was tremendous intellectual ferment throughout the known world during this time. Not only do we see the genesis of philosophy in that part of the world known as Ancient Greece, but the sixth century B.C. was also the century that witnessed the birth of Zoroastrianism (Zoroaster, a.k.a. Zarathustra, 660–583 B.C.) in Persia, Buddhism (Gautama Buddha, 563–483 B.C.) in India, and Taoism (Lao Tse, 604–531 B.C.) and Confucianism (Confucius, 551–479 B.C.) in China. For the first time in the history of man, the ultimate questions (What is man? What is the world? What is truth, goodness, beauty?) were extracted from a purely religious context. With the emergence of Western philosophy and even some forms of Eastern mysticism there was a gradual shift from appeals to external authority and tradition to reliance on personal experience and logical reasoning. This distinction between faith and reason became the dominant issue for the great psychologists of the Middle Ages (Chapter 2).

The Renaissance (Chapter 2) witnessed a further dissociation of reason and experience from belief and authority as evidenced within the Church by the Reformation as well as by a growing intellectual class who were not clerics. The Renaissance served as a necessary prelude to the seventeenth century (Chapter 3) and the emergence of modern philosophy, which gave birth to modern science where the appeal would be to knowledge acquired through the senses and eventually to controlled observation and experimentation. The eighteenth century (Chapter 4) was the period of the great metaphysical psychologists who prepared the way for the final emancipation of psychology from philosophy. With the maturation of physiology in the early nineteenth century (Chapter 5), the stage was set for the birth of experimental psychology in the later half of the nineteenth century with the opening of the first psychological laboratories in Europe and America and the emergence of the great schools of psychology in the early twentieth century (Chapter 6). Finally, there is a separate treatment of the development of clinical psychology from its roots in psychiatry (Chapter 7).

CHAPTER ONE

Classical Antiquity

A. THE PRE-SOCRATICS (600–450 B.C.)

These men were the first philosophers. They are important to the history of psychology because they attempted to ask the old questions about the ultimate nature of things in an entirely new context, one that stressed reason and observation rather than myth and religion in the pursuit of truth and wisdom—thus the term *philosophy.**

The Pre-Socratics were concerned primarily with ontology (what is the basic stuff of all reality?) and cosmology (how did the world begin and what is its structure?). For the most part, these men were espousers of monism, i.e., the theory that there is only one ultimate principle of reality rather than two, which is dualism. The majority of Pre-Socratics were also believers in *hylozoism,* a theory about the ultimate nature of reality that fails to distinguish between animate and inanimate and thus concludes that all matter is alive.

Thales (640?–546 B.C.)—Father of Philosophy

Taught that water is the ultimate stuff of reality.

---

*A word in *italics* indicates further treatment in the Glossary (Section III). A name printed in **boldface** indicates a thinker who is given a separate entry.

Anaximander (611–547 B.C.)

1. Argued that the "boundless" or "infinite" is the ultimate nature of reality. (Some historians see a similarity between this "boundlessness" and the contemporary concept of "energy.")

2. Wrote what is probably the first philosophical work, *peri physis* ("On Nature").

Anaximenes (588–524 B.C.)

Argued that air is the ultimate substance of reality.

Pythagoras (572?–497? B.C.) — Father of Mathematics

1. Reported to have taught a dualism of body and mind, but nevertheless believed that number was the ultimate principle of reality.

2. Believed in the immortality of the soul and the doctrine of transmigration (a form of reincarnation).

3. Is credited with coining the term *philosophy,* referring to himself as a "lover of wisdom."

Heraclitus (533?–475 B.C.)

Taught that change, i.e., becoming, is the only reality and that fire is the first principle. ("Into the same river, one cannot step twice.")

Parmenides (fl, 495 B.C.)

Argued against **Heraclitus** that permanence, i.e., being, is the ultimate reality.

Alcmaeon of Croton (fl. 500 B.C.)

1. Reputed to be the first to dissect a human cadaver.

2. The first to make the distinction between perceiving and thinking.

3. The first to locate the soul in the brain.

Anaxagoras (500?–428 B.C.)

The first to posit the existence of mind or reason (*nous*) as necessary to explain the orderliness of the universe.

Empedocles (495?–435 B.C.)

1. Argued that there are four, not one, basic and irreducible cosmic elements: water, air, fire, and earth. Love, or the principle of good, binds these elements together; hate, or the principle of evil, tears them apart.

2. Articulated the first theory of perception, namely, that objects are perceived because they emanate representative "images" of themselves which enter the blood through the pores of the body and produce an awareness of the world outside. (This theory came to be known as the "emanation" theory and was attacked by **J. Müller** as late as the nineteenth century.)

Leucippus (fl. 450 B.C.) — Father of Atomism

The first to radically break from the monism of his predecessors; posited a plurality of ultimate realities, which he called "atoms," material entities, differing in shape and size, and moving in a void of nonbeing.

Protagoras (480?–411? B.C.) — Father of Sophism

1. One of the first to distinguish between the reality of an object in itself (objectivity) and its appearance (subjectivity), giving a primacy to man's perception as implied in the statement, "Man is the measure of all things, of things that are that they are, and of things that are not that they are not."

2. Founder of the Greek school of Sophism, which was characterized by subtle arguments and gave rise to what today we call relativism, i.e., all points of view are equally valid, and there is no absolute standard of truth.

B. CLASSIC PERIOD OF GREECE (450–300 B.C.)

During this time lived the formulators of the great systems of philosophy that have contributed to the major traditions of Western thought. Though the terminology has changed, the issues that emerged during this time, as well as the solutions, provide psychology, no less than philosophy, with its major controversies to the present day.

Socrates (469–399 B.C.)

1. One of the first thinkers to argue for the importance of self-knowledge. "Know thyself!" and "The unexamined life is not worth living!" are attributed to Socrates by **Plato.**

2. Perhaps best known for what came to be called the Socratic method, a teaching technique employing systematic questioning of the student to reveal his actual ignorance, or, more usually, to elicit a clear definition of some truth that is believed to be implicitly known by all rational beings.

3. Identified virtue with knowledge and taught therefore that ignorance is at the root of all evil and misconduct.

4. One of the first philosophers to be put to death because of his ideas; thus became a martyr to the right of freedom of thought and expression.

Democritus (460?–370 B.C.) — Father of Materialism

1. Further developed the atomistic theory of **Leucippus** and thus became the founder of that tradition in Western thought which reduces all reality to matter and mechanistic terms.

2. Wrote what is probably the first treatise on the soul, *peri psyche* ("On the Soul").

3. Anticipated the concept of sensory threshold with his refinement of **Empedocles'** emanation theory of perception by distinguishing between the density (strength) of the atoms of objects and the body's atoms to account for sensation.

Hippocrates (460?–377 B.C.) — Father of Medicine

1. Articulated a theory of illness, including mental illness, based on whether the four "humors," i.e., bodily fluids (black bile, yellow bile, phlegm, and blood), were in harmonious proportion in the body. (Cf. **Galen,** who developed this concept into a theory of personality.)

2. Described and labeled a number of mental conditions such as euphoria and depression, senile dementia, and

hysteria (which was assumed to be related to dislodgement of the uterus, thus its name).

3. Argued that epilepsy was an organic, not "sacred," disease. (In fact, Hippocrates rejected the popular belief that demonic possession was a cause of mental illness, a belief that has persisted until recent times.)

4. Firmly believed that the functioning of the body can be understood and should not be relegated to the mysterious.

Plato (427–347 B.C.)

1. Articulated the first full-blown dualism, distinguishing between body and mind (soul) or between sensory knowledge and intellectual knowledge. (Plato went so far as to posit a separate world of Ideas or Forms as distinct from the world of everyday experience which is but a "shadow" of the former. This position is known as *Platonic dualism* and is described in the famous "Allegory of the Cave" in the *Republic*.)

2. Believed, with **Alcmaeon**, that the brain is the seat of the soul.

3. Following **Pythagoras**, believed in the immortality of the soul.

4. Explained knowledge through the doctrine of reminiscence, i.e., the soul's remembering of an idealized previous existence, leading to a position known as *nativism*.

5. While affirming the essential unity of the soul, Plato distinguished three aspects: the cognitive (reason), the conative (what Plato called the "spirited" and what we would call the will), and the appetitive (desire).

6. Wrote the first Utopia (an imaginary ideal society), *The Republic*, in which he proposed a kind of aristocratic communism as the best form of government.

Aristotle (384–322 B.C.) — Father of Psychology*

1. Wrote the first systematic discussion of the soul in his

---

*Understood here is metaphysical or philosophical psychology, not to be confused with the scientific or experimental psychology of **Wundt** and his successsors.

peri psyche ("On the Soul").

2. Attempted to correct what he felt was the exaggerated dualism of **Plato** with a body-mind theory that came to be known as *hylomorphism*. This theory stated that everything is constituted by two fundamental principles: prime matter and substantial form, neither of which can exist independently of the other, in contrast to Plato's concept of Idea or Form.

3. Took a moderate position on the origin of human knowledge (between the implied *sensationism* of the Pre-Socratics and the *rationalism* of Plato) which came to be known as *empiricism,* i.e., all knowledge is derived from experience.

4. Presented the first description and interpretation of human experience and behavior in concrete (even modern) terms: learning and memory; occult phenomena; emotion; self-control and interpersonal relations; sensation and the five senses; psychology of youth and old age; drama and the theory of catharsis.

5. The first to articulate the concept of association to explain memory, specifically the principles of contiguity (sequence in time), similarity, contrast, frequency, emotional effect, and degree of meaningfulness.

6. Sometimes referred to as the first historian of psychology, because without Aristotle's references we would know very little about the Pre-Socratics.

7. Believed that the heart was the seat of the soul.

8. Advanced the concept of *teleology,* the idea that there is purpose or design in nature, and thus opposed the *mechanism* of the Atomists, **Leucippus** and **Democritus.**

C. HELLENISTIC PERIOD (300–100 B.C.)

As a result of Alexander's (356–323 B.C.) conquest of the known world, the great systems of the Classical Period of Greece began to "Hellenize" (render Greek-like) the rest of the world, with its center in Alexandria. Only a few philosopher-psychologists emerged during this time who are important for the history of psychology.

Theophrastus (371?–287? B.C.)

Disciple of **Aristotle,** perhaps best known for his collection of thirty personality sketches or character types, titled *Characters,* which is seen by historians as a precursor of the many psychological typologies that appeared later, particularly in the nineteenth and early twentieth centuries.

Epicurus (342–270 B.C.) — Father of Epicureanism

Subscribed to a form of hedonistic ethics that favored intellectual pleasure over the merely physical and recognized the importance of moderation and virtue in the pursuit of happiness.

Zeno the Stoic (335–265 B.C.) — Father of Stoicism

1. Argued that man's ethical obligation is to live rationally, without passion, and in accordance with the inherent Reason in the world, accepting whatever fate may bring; thus, Stoicism came to be identified with a kind of impassiveness or indifference, especially to pain and suffering.

2. Argued for a relative freedom in man, at least insofar as man has the power to determine his mental attitude toward what life may bring.

3. One of the first Western thinkers to develop a doctrine of *pantheism.*

Erasistratus (304?–250? B.C.) — Father of Physiology*

The first to distinguish between sensory and motor nerves, but the distinction was lost until the nineteenth century when it was rediscovered by Charles Bell (1774–1842) and François Magendie (1783–1855).

D. GRAECO-ROMAN PERIOD (100 B.C.–400 A.D.)

During this time, the Roman Empire conquered the Hellenic

---

*Understood here as nonexperimental physiology and not to be confused with the science of physiology that emerged in the eighteenth century.

world, and the two Hellenistic philosophies of Stoicism and Neo-Platonism vied with each other for dominance. A third force began to make an impact upon Western thought during this period, namely Christianity, which is represented here by two of the Church Fathers.

Galen (130–200)

1. Known as the first experimental physiologist because of the accuracy of his observations in anatomy and physiology based upon dissection of animal corpses.

2. Articulated a theory of temperaments, based on **Hippocrates'** four humors, that became the first theory of personality. The four temperaments were: melancholic (excess of black bile), phlegmatic (phlegm), choleric (yellow bile), and sanguine (blood).

Plotinus (205–270) — Father of Neo-Platonism

1. Attempted to integrate the doctrines of **Plato** and **Aristotle** with Oriental conceptions of the world viewed as an emanation from the One, with which the human soul struggles to regain communion, occasionally experienced as ecstacy in this life.

2. One of the first thinkers to articulate a concept of self-consciousness, which anticipated **Locke's** "reflection" and **Wundt's** "introspection."

St. Augustine (354–430)

Probably the greatest of the Church Fathers, frequently known as the "First Modern Psychologist," because of his acute powers of introspection and self-analysis as manifested in his *Confessions,* the first of a long tradition in this genre.

E. THE DARK AGES (400–1000)

The intellectual light of Western thought cast a dim shadow during this time and would have flickered out were it not for the Jewish and Arab scholars who kept alive the classical tradition for its eventual renascence in the Middle Ages. No psychologists of consequence lived during this time.

CHAPTER TWO

The Middle Ages and the Renaissance

A. THE MIDDLE AGES (1000–1450)

This was the time when the great schools of Europe were founded and the ensuing "Scholasticism" emerged as the dominant philosophy of the West until the seventeenth century. Scholasticism was an outgrowth of the philosophy of the Church Fathers that rediscovered **Aristotle** and sought to bolster Christian dogma by demonstrating its reasonableness.

Roger Bacon (1214–1294)

Important for the history of psychology because he advocated the use of observation and induction in addition to deductive reasoning, at a time when appeal to authority and tradition was the only acknowledged manner of correct thinking.

St. Thomas Aquinas (1225–1274)

1. Considered by most historians to be the greatest philosopher of the Middle Ages; argued successfully for the acceptance of **Aristotle** by the Church and the position that there is but *one* truth, i.e., there is no inherent contradiction between revelation (faith) and reason.

2. Laid the foundations for what came to be known as "faculty psychology," i.e., the view that the soul possesses dif-

ferent faculties or powers (sensitive, vegetative, locomotive, and rational) and through its "informing" the body (*hylomorphism*) carries out its functions.

B. THE RENAISSANCE (1450–1600)

This period is usually known as a transitional time in Europe between the Middle Ages and the seventeenth century, characterized by a humanistic revival of the classical influence as reflected in the flowering of the arts and literature as well as by the emergence of modern science.

Paracelsus (1493–1541)

1. A physician who rejected demonic possession as the cause of mental illness at a time when the Inquisition was condemning people to death for possession by the devil and witchcraft.

2. Usually credited with the suggestion of a concept that anticipated **Freud**'s notion of unconscious motivation.

Vives (1492–1540)

1. Perhaps of all the Renaissance philosophers, Vives best typifies the transitional period between Scholasticism and the modern period beginning with the seventeenth century. Vives attacked the formalism of Scholasticism and anticipated the modern view with his emphasis on induction as the source of truth and his insistence on usefulness as the test of the value of knowledge (cf. *pragmatism*).

2. Anticipated the law of conditioning ("When an animal enjoys something at the sound of a tone, then when the tone is heard, it will expect the object it enjoyed previously.").

Francis Bacon (1561–1626)

1. Stood at the crossroads between the Renaissance and the seventeenth century; a great systematizer and organizer of what would become a new way of knowing. With the publication of *The New Organon of the Sciences* (1620), Bacon issued a formal declaration of independence for induction

and experimentation insofar as they contributed to the emancipation of man's thinking from metaphysical analysis and deduction.

2. Perhaps best known is Bacon's classification of prejudices or sources of human error in philosophy and science, which he called Idols: A. Idols of the Cave—personal prejudices and mental defects; B. Idols of the Tribe—ethnocentric customs of the human race; C. Idols of the Market Place—ill-defined use of words; D. Idols of the Theater—unwarranted reliance on authority figures and tradition.

CHAPTER THREE

The Seventeenth Century

With the seventeenth century there emerged a new way of perceiving reality and thus a new way of perceiving man. The central metaphysical question was whether the soul (and therefore the mind) differed from the body and if so, how. For sixteen centuries, Christian philosophy argued for the immortality of the soul and therefore its "higher" essence than the mortal body's. In **Descartes** a new alternative was suggested, a dualism that depended not on the immortality of the soul but on the psychological characteristics of the mind, which differed from all else because of its capacity to think, to doubt everything but its own existence, and therefore to be aware of itself.

The other major development during this time was also a consequence of this new dualism. Belief and opinion gave way to observation and experience in a radical way, and it was a short leap from this implicit *empiricism* to controlled observation and eventually to systematic intervention; thus a new methodology, experimentation, was born and modern science was established.

Thomas Hobbes (1588–1679) — Father of Social Psychology

1. Anticipated the British School of Empiricism by arguing that the mind contains nothing but what has been derived from experience, an idea as old as **Aristotle** but radical in Hobbes's time.

2. Espoused a form of materialism by arguing that all reality is reducible to matter and motion.

3. One of the first moderns, following **Protagoras** and **Democritus,** to distinguish between the qualities of experience and what is inherent in things themselves, anticipating **Locke's** distinction between primary and secondary qualities of objects.

4. Reestablished Aristotle's doctrine of the association of ideas, which was to blossom into the *associationism* of **Hartley** in the eighteenth century.

5. Developed the concept of the "social contract" in his *Leviathon* (1651) to explain why men opt for a state, namely, for self-protection in spite of the human condition, which was "each one for himself."

6. Derived from this cynical view of human nature, namely that self-interest is the basis of human conduct, is what came to be known as "psychological hedonism," as developed by Jeremy Bentham (1748–1832) and **Freud.**

René Descartes (1596–1650) — Father of Modern Philosophy and Father of Physiological Psychology

1. Represented the beginning of a new era in the history of ideas because he was the first thinker to clearly identify the soul with consciousness and was therefore the first philosopher of the self. Deduced the self's existence from the mind's ability to think, *"Cogito, ergo sum."*

2. Articulated a theory of "innate ideas," following **Plato,** i.e., the mind contains principles or capacities for knowing things (such as God, self, mathematics, geometry, space and time), for which experience provides an occasion for their becoming actually known. The theory eventually led to the doctrine of *nativism.*

3. Proposed a dualistic body-mind theory known as *interactionism,* namely that the soul interacts with the body through the pineal gland, the only organ of the brain that is not bilateral. Though the theory quickly fell into disrepute as a solution of the problem, Descartes elevated the problem itself to such importance that no philosopher has been able to ignore it since.

4. One of the first philosopher-psychologists to articulate

the concept of "reflex," i.e., an unlearned, quasi-mechanical response to narrowly defined stimuli, although Descartes's examples would not be acceptable today.

5. Advanced one of the first psychological theories of the emotions, reducing the diversity of man's feeling life to six basic "passions": joy, sadness, love, hate, wonder, and desire.

Baruch Spinoza (1632–1677)

1. Argued against the dualism of **Descartes** by positing that there is only one substance (*monism*) and that substance is God (*pantheism*).

2. Solved the body-mind problem by suggesting that they are aspects of the same reality but exist in a *parallel* fashion. This concept is reflected in the *parallelism* of **Leibniz** but differs in its insistence on *monism*.

3. One of the first moderns to espouse psychological *determinism,* which argued against the concept of man's inherent freedom.

John Locke (1632–1704) — Father of British Empiricism

1. Espoused the notion that all knowledge comes from the senses (and reflection or introspection, which he called the "inner sense") and that man is a *tabula rasa* (blank slate) at birth, a theory of knowledge that became known as *empiricism* and was opposed to the *rationalism* of **Descartes, Spinoza,** and **Leibniz.**

2. One of the first to make the distinction between primary and secondary sensible qualities of objects: primary qualities are said to exist in the thing itself independent of the observer (e.g., size, motion, shape), whereas secondary qualities do not actually exist in the thing itself but give rise to sensations within the perceiver (e.g., color, taste, heat, and cold).

Sir Isaac Newton (1642–1727)

1. Regarded as one of the greatest scientists of all times, Newton bolstered the scientific method by grounding it in mathematics.

2. The first to posit what came to be known as scientific

determinism, the theory that all events are determined by preceding causes, a premise on which much of modern science is based.

Gottfried Leibniz (1646–1716)

1. Developed an alternative body-mind theory to **Descartes** known as *preestablished harmony:* the body and mind are synchronized with each other by God, appearing to interact but not in fact doing so. This theory was eventually detheologized and emerged in the nineteenth century as *psychophysical parallelism,* the predominant body-mind theory to this day.

2. Suggested that consciousness is a continuum ranging in degree of clarity from *petites perceptions* (what might now be called the unconscious) through perception (awareness of outer objects) to *apperception* (awareness of self), a term coined by Leibniz himself.

CHAPTER FOUR

The Eighteenth Century

Dubbed by Whitehead the "Century of Rationalism," the eighteenth century is more frequently referred to by historians as the period of the Enlightenment. In this century, stimulated by the intellectual ferment of the seventeenth, the value of man's reason reached its apex as superior to all traditional beliefs and values. There was renewed faith in individual man, in the ideal of universal progress, and in the newly emerging sciences. Psychology would have to wait until the nineteenth century before it reached its maturity and emancipated itself from the benign parentage of philosophy. However, with the focus on man and his wonderful mind and body, psychology was advancing and some of the greatest philosophers of this century were also astute psychologists. For the first time, elaborate psychological theories were beginning to appear to explain the problem of knowledge.

George Berkeley (1685–1753)—Father of Subjective Idealism
   1. Wrote what is considered by most historians to be the first psychological monograph, *Essay toward a Theory of Vision* (1709), an empirical explanation of space perception as acquired through the association of elementary sensations of sight and touch.
   2. Recognizing the subjectivism implicit in Lockean empiricism, Berkeley argued that our experience is nothing more than a collection of impressions and ideas, positing God as

the guarantor that our sensations are constant and dependable, and positing the soul as the source of the unity of our experience. (Though Berkeley called his doctrine "mentalism," it matured into *subjective idealism* and laid the cornerstone of modern metaphysical idealism.)

Christian von Wolff (1679–1754) — Father of Modern Faculty Psychology

1. Developed an updated version of medieval "faculty psychology" that represented an antagonism to the emerging empirical "blank slate" view of man and continues to the present day in the form of *nativism*.

2. The first to distinguish between "empirical psychology" and "rational psychology" in 1734, an indication that psychology was beginning to aspire toward becoming a bona fide science.

David Hartley (1705–1757) — Father of British School of Associationism

Provided the doctrine of *associationism* with a physiological basis and thus transformed it into one of the first psychological theories of thought and action, which contributed substantively to the emergence of *psychophysical parallelism* as the dominant body-mind position of the nineteenth and early twentieth centuries. (Hartley's specific notion of sensations based upon "vibrations" within the nervous system quickly became obsolete, but the grounding of a theory of thought and action in a physiological explanation contributed to the eventual separation of psychology from philosophy.)

Thomas Reid (1710–1796) — Father of the Scottish School (School of Common Sense)

1. Reacted against the *skepticism* of **Hume** by arguing for a return to "common sense" and the everyday experience of the man-in-the-street (*naive realism*).

2. The first to clearly distinguish between sensation as the raw stuff of experience and perception, which carries an in-

evitable reference to an external object that can be known in itself.

David Hume (1711-1776) — Father of Modern Skepticism

1. Took **Berkeley**'s idealism to its logical conclusion and denied the existence of God, the soul, and even the self. Man can know only his experience and thus "true" knowledge is unobtainable (*skepticism*).

2. Rejected the principle of causality as unverifiable from experience alone; described it rather as an acquired habit of thought, and therefore argued for the association of ideas (by contiguity and resemblance) as sufficient explanation for the whole of mental life.

Etienne de Condillac (1715-1780) — Father of Sensationalism

Articulated an extreme version of **Locke**'s *empiricism* in which he reduced all knowledge to experience and all experience to sensation. Perhaps Condillac is best remembered for his illustration of the sentient statue who develops all the mental processes beginning with but a single sense, e.g., smell, demonstrating the superfluity of even the doctrine of association to explain man's mental life.

Immanuel Kant (1724-1804) — Father of Critical Idealism

1. Attempted to forge a synthesis out of the two seemingly irreconcilable dominant philosophies of his time: *rationalism* and *empiricism*. Kant agreed with empiricism that we can know only the "phenomenon" (that which appears) and not the "noumenon" (the thing-in-itself), but he also agreed with rationalism that we experience unity in the act of perception and that we are not simply a *tabula rasa* at birth but are born with a capacity for human experience. This capacity for experience Kant analysed into 12 a priori (before the fact) "transcendental categories" (e.g., causality, unity, existence) and the two "intuitions" of space and time; these delineate the context in which Nature must occur in order to be intelligible.

2. Kant had direct impact on the emergence of psychology in two ways. First, Kant gave psychology its early quantitative

bias by his insistence that mathematics is the basis of scientific knowledge because of its a priori status. Second, in ironic fashion, Kant delayed the birth of psychology as a science because he argued that the data of psychology, namely, mental processes, do not have extension (only time) and therefore are not measurable. For example, a feeling has duration but does not exist in space. In other words, Kant believed that psychology could not be a science because its data are one-dimensional (temporal) and science needs data that occur in both space and time in order to be treated mathematically.

3. Extended the concept of *apperception* to describe the mind's constant organizing of experience in order to achieve the unity of perception.

CHAPTER FIVE

The Early Nineteenth Century

Though the eighteenth century saw the birth of experimental psychology, the last of the great "metaphysical psychologists" appear in the early part of this century. An important development of this period is the birth of experimental physiology as an independent science, which paved the way for psychology. Another important development is the growing acceptance of the theory of evolution by the scientific community, brought about primarily by the impressive evidence produced by Darwin and others.

Jean-Baptiste Lamarck (1744–1829)
1. Espoused a theory of organic evolution based on the doctrine of the "inheritance of acquired characteristics," i.e., environmental conditions induce structural changes (adaptations) in animals and plants that are then genetically transmitted to offspring.
2. Suggested a related theory to account for organic evolution, namely the existence of an inherent tendency in living things towards greater complexity (*teleology*). This Aristotelian idea of an inherent, purposive principle, which was deduced from certain biological phenomena, exerted an influence on the *hormic* psychology of **McDougall.**

Herbert Spencer (1820–1903)
Introduced evolutionary theory (in fact coined the term

"evolution" in 1852) to psychology and applied it to mental life. Defined intelligence as adaptation to the environment and thereby influenced the development of genetic (developmental) psychology and comparative psychology.

Charles Darwin (1809–1882) — Father of Evolutionism

1. Though not the first to articulate a theory of evolution, Darwin was the first to supply the empirical and persuasive evidence for a theory of the origin and perpetuation of new forms of animal and plant life. The predominant mechanism, according to Darwin, was "natural selection," the perpetuation of successful adaptations and the elimination of unsuccessful ones by the competition among organisms for limited food supplies.

2. Kept a diary of his infant son, which he began in 1840 but did not publish until 1877. This was the first of the so-called "baby biographies," which contributed to the emergence of child psychology in the following decade.

3. Articulated one of the first scientific theories of the emotions in 1872, arguing for the instinctive nature of the emotions, and demonstrated their biological utility in the perpetuation of the species.

Franz Gall (1758–1828) — Father of Phrenology

Founded one of the first personality theories that argued for a correlation between bodily configuration (in this case, conformations of the skull) and personality traits (37 in all). Though the theory enjoyed widespread popularity, it was eventually discredited. However, its emphasis on the importance of precise measurement and implied localization of cortical functions contributed significantly to the historical development of psychology.

Johann F. Herbart (1776–1841) — Father of Educational Psychology

1. Constructed the last great system of metaphysical psychology, which he defined as a "science based on experience, metaphysics, and mathematics."

2. Developed a systematic theory of the conscious and the unconscious, from which he derived the concept of "threshold of consciousness" to explain memory and forgetting.

3. Perhaps best remembered for his concept of *apperceptive mass,* i.e, the residue that accumulates in the unconscious from past experience and that contributes to the assimilation and transformation of new perceptions.

4. Became interested in pedagogy and demonstrated the relevance of psychology for education, particularly through the so-called Herbartian Steps of Instruction: (1) Preparation; (2) Presentation; (3) Association; (4) Generalization; (5) Application.

Thomas Brown (1778–1820)

Ironically, though affiliated with the Scottish School founded by **Reid** and whose *raison d'etre* was opposition to *associationism,* Brown is best known for his nine secondary laws of association (which he called "suggestion"), of which the first four are the most important: (1) duration (of the original stimulus), (2) liveliness, (3) frequency, and (4) recency.

Sir William Hamilton (1788–1856)

Combined the thought of the Scottish School and German Idealism into a system that argued against *associationism.* This view is perhaps best exemplified by Hamilton's original concept of "redintegration" for explaining memory: "tendency of an impression to bring back into consciousness the whole experience of which it was at one time a part."

Adolphe Quetelet (1796–1874) — Father of Modern Statistics

1. In his book, *Sur l'homme* ("On Man") (1835), Quetelet argued for a statistical probability basis for the social sciences and developed the concept of the "average man," the theoretical construct which falls at the center of the normal curve for all human characteristics.

2. Coined the term "statistics."

Auguste Comte (1798–1857)—Father of Positivism

Propounded the theory of *positivism,* which indirectly influenced psychology by challenging it to become a bona fide science and argued against introspection as a legitimate scientific method.

Ernst H. Weber (1795–1878)

1. Developed a metric for the measurement of sensory stimuli, the "just noticeable difference (j.n.d.)," that suggested the possibility for objectification of man's psychological response to his environment.

2. Discovered what came to be known as "Weber's Law": the just noticeable difference between sensations in the same sense modality is detected when the original stimulus is increased by a constant fraction of itself. (For example, Weber determined that perception of weight has a ratio of 1/30 and therefore an increase in weight is perceptible only when it is at least 1/30 of the original weight.)

Gustav Fechner (1801–1887)—Father of Psychophysics

1. Developed a science of measuring the magnitude of sensation, which Fechner termed "psychophysics," and thus paved the way for the eventual development of a science of the mind.

2. Articulated the relationship between the magnitude of the stimulus and the magnitude of the response (sensation), which came to be known as "Fechner's Law": when stimuli increase by a constant ratio, the sensations aroused by them increase by equal increments or steps. (The formula is $S = K \log R$, where S is the magnitude of the sensory response measured from the absolute threshold as zero; R is the magnitude of the stimulus measured with the absolute threshold as a unit; and K is an appropriate constant derived from Weber's Law, e.g., 1/30 in the case of weight discrimination.) Another version of Fechner's Law is: As a stimulus varies geometrically, the sensation varies arithmetically.

3. Posited a unique solution to the body-mind problem, known as *panpsychism,* which resembled Jainism of India in its espousal of spirit or life in all of nature.

Johannes Müller (1801–1858) — Father of Experimental Physiology*

1. Occupied the first chair of physiology at the University of Berlin in 1833 and wrote the first great textbook of physiology, *Elements of Physiology* (1833–1840), which became an international classic for several decades.

2. Perhaps best remembered for his espousal in 1826 of the theory of the "specific energies of nerves," which held that each sensory nerve carries but one kind of quality or experience; optical nerves carry only visual impressions, etc. Although this theory has been disproved, it should be noted that Müller considered the possibility that the specific qualities might also be explained by different terminations in the brain, a view that anticipates the theory of cortical localization.

James Mill (1773–1836) — Father of Mental Mechanics

Developed a doctrine of radical *associationism* known as "mental mechanics," in which simple ideas become complex through rigid, mechanical processes in accordance with the principle of contiguity alone.

John Stuart Mill (1806–1873) — Father of Mental Chemistry

1. Son of **James Mill,** he rejected his father's teaching and posited in its place the doctrine of "mental chemistry," arguing by analogy with chemical bonding that complex ideas have properties that cannot be reduced to those of their components, or "the whole is greater than the sum of its parts," as the Gestaltists would argue later on.

2. Published in 1843 the first systematic presentation of the

---

*Some historians feel this title should be shared with Albrecht von Haller (1708–1777).

"canons" of experimental inquiry: agreement, difference, joint method, concomitant variations, and residues.

Alexander Bain (1818–1903)

1. Considered to be the last great philosophical psychologist of Britain as was **Herbart** of Germany. His books *The Senses and the Intellect* (1855) and *The Emotions and the Will* (1859) were *the* textbooks in psychology in the English language for almost 50 years.

2. Founded the first journal of psychology, *Mind,* in 1876, though it was somewhat philosophical in orientation.

Gregor Mendel (1822–1884) — Father of Modern Genetics

Conducted experiments and articulated the now accepted theory of trait transmission known as Mendel's Law in 1866, which was ignored and forgotten until rediscovered and publicized by Hugo De Vries (1848–1935) in 1900.

Rudolph Lotze (1817–1881)

1. Most significant contribution to the history of psychology was through his eminent students while holding the chair of philosophy at Göttingen (1844–1881): **Brentano, Stumpf,** and **G. E. Müller.**

2. Perhaps best known for his famous "local signs" theory of visual space perception and cutaneous sensitivity, espousing an empirical position: psychological space is built up through distinctive sensations of the various parts of the sense receptor and is mediated by corresponding muscular sensations to produce the resultant experience. This theory led to the first enunciation of the doctrine of *isomorphism.*

Hermann von Helmholtz (1821–1894)

1. The first to measure the speed of conduction of the nerve impulse in 1850. (Found it to be 30 meters per second in a frog's leg — modern methods show it to be approximately 120 meters per second.)

2. Conducted the first reaction time experiment.

3. Developed and clarified Thomas Young's (1733–1829)

theory of color vision into the Young-Helmholtz theory, the so-called three-fiber theory. This theory postulated that there are three different kinds of fibers in the retina which produce sensations of red, green, and violet respectively, combinations of which produce all of the other colors, a theory still viable today.

4. Proposed the still viable "resonance theory" (also known as the "place theory") of hearing, namely that fibers of the basilar membrane act as resonators, different fibers being responsive to different frequencies.

5. Developed a notion of "unconscious inference" as it influences perception, a highly contemporary concept.

Franciscus Donders (1818–1889)

The first to recognize the significance of reaction time as a way of measuring psychological processes, which Donders termed "mental chronometry." Specifically, Donders extended the simple reaction time experiment of Helmholtz to include discrimination and choice.

Evald Hering (1834–1918)

1. Espoused a theory of color vision in 1878 that rivaled the Young-Helmholtz theory; it was based on four primary colors (red, green, blue, and yellow) plus black and white.

2. Argued for a nativistic theory of visual space perception in opposition to the empiristic theories of **Lotze, Helmholtz,** and **Wundt.**

CHAPTER SIX

Experimental Psychology of the Nineteenth and Early Twentieth Centuries

Most historians agree that experimental psychology was born in 1879 when **Wundt** opened his psychological laboratory at the University of Leipzig in Germany. Although there is some evidence that **James**'s laboratory at Harvard antedated Wundt's by four years, it simply was too "pocket-sized," as one historian (Roback, 1952) has put it, to deserve the honor. The fact is that students came from all over the world, including America, to study at Wundt's laboratory not James's. Nonetheless, America was ripe for this new science and in only twenty years after James's inauspicious beginnings at Harvard there were twenty-four psychological laboratories scattered throughout the United States. Within a period of several decades, there emerged the major "schools" of American psychology: *Functionalism, Structuralism, Gestaltism, Behaviorism, Hormic* (Purposive) *Psychology,* and *Dynamic Psychology,* all of which continue to feed the mainstream of experimental psychology in America today, although few schools continue to claim strict adherents.

This chapter includes the major experimental psychologists grouped according to the country in which they lived their professional lives from Wundt up to the founders of the various schools of the early twentieth century, as well as a few others, both physiologists and philosophers, who influenced the early stages of the development of experimental psychology. Psychiatry and clinical psychology receive a separate treatment in the seventh and final chapter.

A. GERMANY

Wilhelm Wundt (1833-1920) — Father of Experimental Psychology

1. Opened the first psychological laboratory at the University of Leipzig in 1879.

2. Taught the first course in experimental psychology at the University of Heidelberg in 1867.

3. Wrote the first textbook in experimental psychology, *Principles of Physiological Psychology* (1873-1874).

4. Defined psychology as the "science of immediate experience" and focused on what he called the "contents of the consciousness": sensations, images, feelings, and combinations through *apperception* and "creative synthesis," access to which was gained through the rigorous technique of *introspection*. This focus on the "contents" or structure of consciousness contained the seeds of what came to be called *structuralism* by **Titchener,** one of Wundt's most loyal students.

5. Reported by one historian (Boring, 1950) to have published an average of 2.7 pages a day throughout his 68 year career (1853-1920), he was one of the most prolific and industrious psychologists who ever lived.

6. Founded the first psychological journal in German, *Philosophische Studien,* in 1881.

Franz Brentano (1838-1917) — Father of Act Psychology

A laicized Catholic priest who, steeped in Scholastic philosophy, argued that mind consists of acts rather than the "contents" that **Wundt** espoused, all of which psychical activity is an expression of intentionality. Brentano's extraordinary book, *Psychology from an Empirical Standpoint* (1874) was published in the same year as **Wundt's** monumental *Principles* *of Physiological Psychology* and acted as a counterweight to **Wundt's** *structuralism*. Brentano was perhaps most influential through his eminent students: **Stumpf, Husserl, von Ehrenfels,** and **Freud,** and is said to be a precursor to **James** and his *functional* psychology.

Ernst Mach (1838-1916)

Laid the foundations for the distinction between independent and dependent experience and thus concluded that physics and psychology are both grounded in experience but from differing points of view, a position known as *epistemological dualism,* to be distinguished from the *metaphysical dualism* that posits two ultimate realities.

Carl Stumpf (1842-1936) — Father of Psychology of Music

1. Espoused a position of *nativism* with **Hering** against the empiricism of **Helmholtz** and **Wundt** and influenced psychology primarily through two of his most famous students, **Wertheimer** and **Husserl,** while holding the chair of philosophy at the University of Berlin, one of the prestigious German universities that rivaled **Wundt's** Leipzig.

2. His *Tonpsychologie* (1883-1890) was the first book written on the psychology of music and tone, in which Stumpf proposed a theory of fusion to explain consonance and dissonance in music. According to Stumpf, two tones are judged consonant to the degree that they "fuse" into a single tone.

Wilhelm Preyer (1842-1897) — Father of Child Psychology*

Wrote the first empirical book on the study of the child, *The Mind of the Child,* in 1881, considered to be the first textbook of child psychology.

Georg E. Müller (1850-1934)

1. Invented the memory drum apparatus with Friedrich

---

*Title shared with James **Baldwin.**

Schumann (1863-1940) in 1893.

2. Standardized the level of difficulty of **Ebbinghaus**'s nonsense syllables.

3. Argued for a more active and dynamic conception of the mind against the more mechanical conception of **Ebbinghaus**, investigating such phenomena as "anticipatory set."

4. One of the early exponents of psychophysical *isomorphism*.

Hermann Ebbinghaus (1850-1909)

1. Conducted the first systematic experimental investigation of learning and forgetting in 1885, specifically serial learning.

2. Introduced to the experimental method in psychology the statistical refinement of eliminating variable errors by numerous observations (repeated measurements).

3. Created the "nonsense syllable" to eliminate the problem of meaning in measuring memory, e.g., ceg, dac.

4. Introduced the standardization of rate of presentation into the learning experiment (Ebbinghaus himself used 2/5 second per syllable).

5. Determined the "curve of forgetting" to be a positive *J*-curve with virtually minimum retention after the fifth day.

6. Discovered the phenomenon of "savings," i.e., the reduction in the amount of time needed to relearn previously learned material, known today as "overlearning."

7. Determined that "spaced" practice is more efficient for learning than "massed" practice.

8. Cofounded the second psychological journal in German with Arthur König (1856-1901), *Zeitschrift für Psychologie und Physiologie der Sinnesorgane,* in 1890.

9. Developed the so-called "Completion Test" in 1897, a series of sentences with a word or phrase left out in each; this technique led to the development of analogies as a way of testing intelligence.

Edmund Husserl (1859-1938) — Father of Phenomenology

Developed **Brentano**'s Act Psychology into an independent

school of philosophy that he defined as a "systematic investigation of phenomena, or conscious experiences, especially as they occur immediately in experience without implications." *Phenomenology* is the descriptive study of experience whereas psychology seeks to explain experience in terms of cause and effect; thus in any psychological investigation, phenomenological analysis would logically precede experimentation.

Christian von Ehrenfels (1859–1932)

A student of **Brentano,** von Ehrenfels posited a *Gestaltqualität* (form quality) in 1890, a quality in our experience which cannot be accounted for by the properties of mere sensations, e.g., the melody of a song or the form of a triangle. This finding suggested a new "element" that was not reducible to the sensations, images, or feelings into which **Wundt** analysed consciousness. Though inadequately developed, the concept of a *Gestaltqualität* was a precursor to both the Würzburg School and the *Gestalt* School.

Oswald Külpe (1862–1915) — Father of the Würzburg School

Provided the experimental verification of **Brentano's** distinction between the content of consciousness and the "act" or conscious function, which George Frederick Stout (1860–1944) christened "imageless thought" in 1896. These phenomena were not accounted for by Wundtian analysis and thus the Würzburg School became an antagonist to *structuralism*. The Würzburg School explored the effects of thought and volition on perception and thus introduced such concepts as "task," "set," and "attitude." The Würzburg School was a precursor of Gestalt psychology and, in fact, the latter's founder, **Wertheimer,** took his Ph.D. at Würzburg University in 1904.

Max Wertheimer (1880–1943) — Father of Gestalt Psychology

Published in 1912 a monograph on "apparent movement" or the phi phenomenon, the perception of one moving light instead of two lights alternatively blinking on and off, when the timing is regulated and the distance between the lights is sufficiently close. This was significant at the time because it suggested an aspect of consciousness that was not reducible to the tripartite scheme of **Wundt** (sensations, images, and feelings). This discovery was developed by Wertheimer into the principle of membership character, i.e., the attributes or qualities of the parts are defined by their relation to the whole system in which they are participating. In other words, content depends on context. From this principle emerged many other principles of perceptual organization: proximity, closure, good continuity, reversible ground and figure, common fate, and Pregnanz. Initially, *Gestalt* psychology attacked the reductionism of Wundtian psychology but shifted its focus to the same perceived weakness of *behaviorism,* which it characterized as "brick and mortar" psychology.

Kurt Koffka (1886–1941)

Great systematizer and integrator of all the experimental evidence for *Gestalt* Psychology's point of view. Koffka's book, *The Principles of Gestalt Psychology* (1935), is considered to be one of the best syntheses of the movement.

Wolfgang Köhler (1887–1967)

1. Physiologist and spokesman of the *Gestalt* movement.

2. Articulated the principle of *isomorphism,* a physiological explanation of perception that became identified with the Gestalt movement.

3. Perhaps best known for his research with apes on the Canary Islands during World War I and his positing the notion of "insight" as the explanation of man's reasoning ability against the "trial and error" hypothesis of **Thorndike.**

William Stern (1871–1938)

1. As eminent in psychological testing in Germany as **Binet** was in France, but somewhat superseded by Binet for posterity.

2. Perhaps best known for developing the formula in 1912 for the "mental quotient," which rendered the "mental age" of Binet more meaningful by dividing it by the chronological

age. (Today, we multiply the mental quotient by 100 and the resulting ratio is known as the "intelligence quotient" or IQ.)

B. FRANCE

Theodule Ribot (1835–1916)

Though primarily interested in psychopathology, Ribot was the first to teach a course in experimental psychology at a French university (Sorbonne) in 1885.

Alfred Binet (1857–1911) — Father of Intelligence Testing

1. Commissioned by the French government in 1904 to develop an instrument for identifying children who would not be able to benefit from normal classroom instruction. In 1905, Binet, along with Théodore Simon (1873–1961), published their first intelligence test, which went through two subsequent revisions in 1908 and 1911. This last edition was translated and restandardized on American children by Lewis Terman (1877–1956) in 1916 and published as the "Stanford-Binet," so named because of Terman's academic affiliation.

2. Cofounded the first French psychological laboratory at the Sorbonne (College of Letters at the University of Paris) in 1889 with Henri Beaunis (1830–1921).

3. Cofounded the first French psychological journal, *L'Année Psychologique,* in 1895 with Victor Henri (1872–1940).

C. GREAT BRITAIN

Francis Galton (1822–1911) — Father of Differential Psychology and Father of Psychometrics

1. Published the first modern treatise on the inheritance of mental ability in 1869, *Hereditary Genius,* in which he discussed psychological differences between the sexes and thus laid the groundwork for what came to be known as "differential psychology."

2. Founded the first psychological testing center in the world ("anthropometric laboratory") in 1882, in which he

measured physical and simple psychological characteristics and thus became the first psychometrician (also known as psychometrist).

3. Conducted the first word-association experiment in 1883.

4. First to make extensive use of the questionnaire and the rating scale for psychological purposes in 1883.

5. First to systematically study mental imagery in 1883.

6. Founder of the *eugenics* movement, for which he coined the term.

7. Conducted the first psychological study using twins.

8. Showed the importance of statistical procedures for psychology and developed the concept of correlation as well as the percentile.

James Ward (1843–1925)

Although steeped in the philosophical psychology of **Bain,** Ward attempted to incorporate the experimental spirit that was in the air and even attempted to open a psychological laboratory at Cambridge, but that remained for William H. Rivers (1864–1922) to accomplish in 1897. Perhaps best known for his celebrated article on psychology in the ninth edition (1886) of the *Encyclopedia Brittannica,* in which Ward argued for a dynamic conception of the mind and in doing so challenged the primacy of the associationist tradition and laid the groundwork for *functionalism,* which **James** acknowledged.

George Romanes (1848–1894) — Father of Comparative Psychology

Wrote the first textbook on comparative psychology, *Animal Intelligence* (1882), i.e., the study of animal behavior for purposes of comparison with man. Romanes's approach was characterized by the anecdotal method and was criticized as being heavily *anthropomorphic.*

C. Lloyd Morgan (1852–1936) — Father of Ethology

1. The first to scientifically study animals in their natural

habitat, a study known as "ethology."

2. Articulated what has come to be known as the "Law of Parsimony" or Lloyd Morgan's Canon: the behavior of animals should not be interpreted as reflecting a higher mental process when a simpler one is sufficient.

Karl Pearson (1857–1936)

One of the founders of modern statistics, Pearson developed three of the most important statistical procedures for analysing psychological data: (1) the standard deviation in 1893; (2) the Pearson product-moment correlation coefficient in 1896 [the original theorem for which was actually developed by the French mathematician A. Bravais (1811–1863) in 1846]; and (3) the chi square in 1900.

Charles Spearman (1863–1945) — Father of Factor Analysis

1. Laid the groundwork for the development of the statistical procedure of factor analysis, i.e., the transformation of test scores into the least number of variables ("factors") that are usually not correlated with each other and supposedly explain the total variation of test performance.

2. Articulated what came to be known as the two-factor theory of intelligence: an explanation of human variation in intellectual performance with the positing of a general ability (*g* factor) ordinarily found in all cognitive behavior and specific abilities (*s* factors), which account for the differentiation of specific abilities within an individual.

3. Developed three widely used statistical procedures: (1) the Spearman rank order correlation coefficient; (2) the Spearman-Brown prophecy formula; and (3) the correction for attenuation of the correlation coefficient.

D. RUSSIA

Ivan Sechenov (1829–1905) — Father of Russian Reflexology

Having studied under **Helmholtz** and **J. Müller**, Sechenov concluded that all behavior, both voluntary and involuntary, is reducible to reflexes and that the study of behavior is adequate for an understanding of all psychology. Sechenov anticipated the *behaviorism* of **Watson,** although there is no evidence that Watson was familiar with Sechenov's writing first-hand.

Ivan Pavlov (1849–1936) — Father of Classical Conditioning

A pharmacologist and physiologist who won the Nobel Prize in 1904 for his work on the physiology of digestion. Through serendipity, Pavlov discovered the "conditioned reflex," a response to an inappropriate (conditioned) stimulus because of earlier associations with an adequate (unconditioned) stimulus. For example, a dog began to salivate (parotid reflex) (*CR*) at the sound of the footsteps of his trainer (*CS*) immediately prior to his being fed (*US*). This discovery led to a belief that the higher mental processes could be reduced to a simple paradigm amenable to the modern focus of an objective, rigorous, and quantitative science.

Vladimir Bekhterev (1857–1927)

Independently of **Pavlov,** Bekhterev developed a similar theory of conditioning as well as a psychological system based upon physiology, positing the reflex as the basis of all behavior. This system Bekhterev called "objective psychology" in 1910, which he changed to *"reflexology"* in 1917.

E. UNITED STATES

William James (1842–1910) — Father of American Psychology

1. In contrast to **Wundt's** *structuralism,* James grasped the evolutionary-*functional* approach to psychology and posed the question, "What for?" "My thinking is first, last, and always for the sake of my doing."

2. Laid some claim to having established the first psychological laboratory in America at Harvard University in 1875.

3. Wrote what is considered one of the greatest textbooks

in psychology, *The Principles of Psychology* (1890), still widely read and deemed relevant.

4. Developed one of the first modern theories of the emotions in 1884, followed by an independent researcher, Carl J. Lange (1834–1900), a year later. Both men concluded that emotion is a product (not the cause) of physiological changes, e.g., "We see a bear, run away, tremble, and are afraid." This theory came to be known as the James-Lange Theory.

5. Conducted the first experiment (one of the few James himself conducted) on the "transfer of training" in 1890.

6. Brought respectability to the study of religious and psychical phenomena through the founding of the American Society for Psychical Research in 1884 and the publication of *The Varieties of Religious Experience* in 1902.

7. After relinquishing the psychological laboratory at Harvard to the directorship of **Münsterberg** in 1892, James became more enamored of philosophy and developed the *pragmatism* of Charles S. Peirce (1839–1914) into one of the most popular schools of philosophy that America has ever produced.

G. Stanley Hall (1844–1924) — Father of Genetic Psychology and Father of Adolescent Psychology

1. Established the second American psychological laboratory at Johns Hopkins University in 1883 (after **William James**).

2. Founded the first psychological journal in America, *American Journal of Psychology,* in 1887.

3. Cofounded with **Baldwin** the American Psychological Association in 1892 and served as its first president.

4. Invited **Freud** to make his one visit to America while serving as president of Clark University in 1909.

John Dewey (1859–1952) — Father of Functional Psychology

Though perhaps better known as a philosopher, Dewey's article on the limitations of *reflexology* and his argument for a more active conception of the organism in 1896 is usually cited as the *functionalist* manifesto, which eventually led to the Chicago School under the tutelage of James R. Angell (1869–1949) and Harvey A. Carr (1873–1954).

James McKeen Cattell (1860–1944) — Father of Applied Psychology*

1. First American to acquire the Ph.D. in psychology in 1886 at the University of Leipzig under **Wundt**.

2. Occupied the world's first chair of psychology at the University of Pennsylvania in 1887.

3. Coined the term "mental test" in 1890.

4. Opened the third psychological laboratory in America at the University of Pennsylvania in 1888.

5. Founded Psychological Corporation, a nonprofit agency for the promotion of applied psychology, in 1921 after being fired from Columbia University for speaking out against the Congressional decision to send conscientious objectors to fight in World War I.

6. Developed the first frequency table of the English language as part of a free association experiment with Sophie Bryant (1850–1922) in 1889, which provided the basis for the Kent-Rosanoff Table in 1910.

James M. Baldwin (1861–1934) — Father of Child Psychology**

1. Influenced by the functionalism contained in Darwin's theory of evolution; extended Ernst Haeckel's (1834–1919) doctrine of recapitulation (organisms pass through stages in the course of maturation that resemble types which have occurred in the evolutionary history of their species) to include the mental development of man from childhood to adulthood.

2. Cofounded with **Hall** the American Psychological Association in 1892.

---

*Title shared with **Münsterberg**.
Title shared with **Preyer.

Hugo Münsterberg (1863-1916) — Father of Applied
  Psychology*
1. Invited by **James** to assume directorship of the
psychological laboratory at Harvard in 1892, after receiving
one of the first Ph.D.s in psychology from **Wundt**'s
laboratory at Leipzig in 1885.
2. Extended psychology into law and industry and wrote
the first textbooks in these areas.

Mary Calkins (1863-1930)
Developed the technique of "paired associates" in the investigation of learning to better study the influence of the so-
called secondary laws of association of **Thomas Brown.**

Edward Titchener (1867-1927) — Father of Structural
  Psychology
An Englishman who brought German psychology to
America, Titchener defined psychology as the study of experience from the point of view of the experiencer, designated
"structural psychology," which was an extension and
simplification of Wundtian psychology. Titchener
distinguished between the object known and the conscious
content of the experience, which is the proper object of
psychology investigated through introspection. This school
began and virtually died with Titchener because of his unwill-
ingness to extend the parameters of psychology beyond those
defined as "structural."

Robert S. Woodworth (1869-1962) — Father of Dynamic
  Psychology
1. Trained in the functional tradition of psychology under
James, Woodworth strove to achieve a synthesis that included
structuralism and *behaviorism* as well, but not what Woodworth felt were the excesses of Watsonian behaviorism. There

---

*Title shared with **Cattell.**

is room for introspection as well as rigorous observations of both animals and man, and since Woodworth emphasized cause and effect, he termed his synthesis, "Dynamic Psychology."

2. Authored the first personality questionnaire in 1919, *Psychoneurotic Inventory,* popularly known as the *Personal Data Sheet,* and used as a screening device for the military in World War I.

William McDougall (1871–1938) — Father of Hormic (Purposive) Psychology

Though he is credited with being the first to define psychology as a science of behavior as early as 1905, McDougall argued for a purposive psychology that was transitional between *functional psychology* and *behaviorism.* He is perhaps best known for his classic *Introduction to Social Psychology* (1908), one of the earliest and most popular textbooks (over 25 editions and printings) that established social psychology as a major branch of psychology. McDougall's theory was that man's behavior is primarily motivated by instincts and is therefore purposive or *hormic* (striving).

Edward L. Thorndike (1874–1949) — Father of Instrumental Learning

1. First to study animal behavior in a laboratory experimentally.

2. Through his study of cats in a "puzzle box," Thorndike achieved experimental verification of "trial and error" learning, so-named by **Bain** in 1855 to distinguish how animals and small children learn from how man learns, which is by reasoning.

3. Discovered that the consequences of an action are more powerful in establishing an association ("connection") than mere contiguity. This finding Thorndike stated in his famous "law of effect": a satisfying outcome increases the likelihood of the same response to a similar situation and conversely, an annoying outcome decreases the likelihood.

4. With **Woodworth** in 1901, conducted a classic experi-

ment on what was termed "transfer of training" in which they concluded against the concept of mental faculties and argued for a strict associationistic view of the mind. This led to Thorndike's rejection of the idea of the mind as an overall mental capacity; he saw it rather as a multitude of particular capacities. For Thorndike, mind became "the number of connections in one's brain." This position led to the multiple-factor theories of L. L. Thurstone (1887-1955) and J. P. Guilford (1897-   ).

5. Wrote the first textbook in educational psychology in 1903, and were it not for **Herbart's** preemption would have earned the title Father of Educational Psychology.

6. Coauthored the famous Thorndike-Lorge list of 30,000 most commonly used words in the English language with their relative frequency of usage, based on written material, in 1944.

John B. Watson (1878-1958) — Father of Behaviorism

1. Authored "Psychology as the Behaviorist Views It" in 1913, a manifesto of American objective psychology and its attendant revolt against *functionalism* as well as *structuralism* and *introspectionism*. In this work and for the rest of his academic career, Watson articulated a position of extreme environmentalism and argued for a redefinition of psychology as a science of behavior as opposed to a science of consciousness or experience.

2. In 1928, wrote *Psychological Care of the Infant and Child,* one of the first psychologically oriented child care books that anticipated Dr. Spock by several decades.

CHAPTER SEVEN

Psychiatry and Clinical Psychology

The history of clinical psychology is the history of psychiatry in its inception, just as the history of experimental psychology is initially the history of philosophy. Most historians date the beginning of modern psychiatry in 1793 when **Pinel** persuaded the Commune during the French Revolution to allow him to remove the chains from the inmates of an insane asylum. This development was followed by the so-called Humanitarian Movement which spread throughout the Western world, thanks mainly to the heroic efforts of **Dorothea Dix.**

The beginnings of clinical psychology are usually dated from 1896 when **Witmer** opened the first clinic in psychology at the University of Pennsylvania. For the most part, clinical psychologists were "test-givers" until World War II when the number of mental patients began to increase significantly in proportion to the number of available psychiatrists. For the first time, clinical psychologists began to do therapy and thus they became therapists as well as "test-givers," while psychiatry became more and more chemotherapeutic in orientation.

A. FRANCE

Phillipe Pinel (1745–1826) — Father of Modern Psychiatry

1. Became the director of the Bicêtre in Paris, an institu-

tion for the insane, in 1792, and literally removed the chains from the inmates incarcerated therein a year later.

2. Developed a more objective and scientific approach to the treatment of mental illness, arguing against the notion of punishment by God and possession by demons.

3. Developed one of the first systems of classifying and diagnosing mental illness according to physical symptoms (nosology).

Jean Esquirol (1772–1840)

Student of and eventual assistant to **Pinel,** Esquirol contributed significantly to the designing of mental hospitals and stressed the importance of record-keeping for understanding the etiology of mental illness.

Jean Itard (1775–1838)

One of the first to engage in educating the mentally retarded, occasioned by his attempt to train a young boy ("feral child") approximately ten years of age, who was found in the forests of Aveyron, France, in 1798. Though Itard despaired after five years of training, the progress made was significant and gave encouragement to his successors, e.g., **Seguin** and Maria Montessori (1870–1952).

Edouard Seguin (1812–1880) — Father of Special Education

1. Developed techniques for the education of the mentally handicapped which came to be known as the "physiological method," emphasizing the importance of training the sensory and motor functions, anticipating modern-day methods.

2. Developed one of the first tests for the identification of mental retardation, known as the "Seguin Form Board," a version of which was incorporated into the Stanford-Binet.

3. Helped to organized the School for Defectives, Randall's Island, New York, in 1850, the first institution of its kind in the world.

Jean Charcot (1825–1893) — Father of Neurology

Established what came to be known as the "School of

Paris" in the controversy with the "School of Nancy" (cf. **Bernheim**) over the nature of hypnosis. Charcot postulated that hypnosis was a physiological phenomenon, related to hysteria and seen as "artificial hysteria." **Freud** studied with Charcot between 1885 and 1886 at La Salpêtrière and referred to him as "my master."

Hippolyte Bernheim (1840–1919)

Cofounder [with Ambroise Liebéault (1823–1904)] of the "School of Nancy" in the controversy with the "Paris School" (cf. **Charcot** and **Janet**) over the nature of hypnosis. Bernheim argued that hypnosis was the suggestion of sleep and differed only in degree from normal consciousness. Bernheim's (1891) book on hypnosis was translated into German by **Freud**.

Pierre Janet (1859–1947) — Father of the School of Dissociation

1. Developed a theory of neurosis based on "dissociation," a splitting of the personality, first proposed in 1887.

2. Coined the term "psychasthenia" (mental weakness) to distinguish from a more serious disturbance known as "neurasthenia."

B. GERMANY AND AUSTRIA

Franz Mesmer (1734–1815) — Father of Hypnotism

Introduced the West to the medical application of what was then known as "animal magnetism," to distinguish it from physical magnetism, the inducing of a trancelike state that eventually came to be known as "mesmerism," and finally "hypnosis," a term coined by James Braid (1795–1860) in 1843 after the Greek god of sleep, Hypnos.

Emil Kraepelin (1856–1926) — Father of Psychopharmacology

1. One of the first to study the effects of drugs (e.g., morphine, ethyl alcohol) on human behavior using the experimen-

tal techniques of the "new" (Wundtian) psychology.

2. Developed a classification system (nosology) of mental disorders in 1883 that provided the basis for present-day psychiatric nomenclature, introducing terms like "manic-depressive" and "paranoia."

Sigmund Freud (1856–1939) — Father of Psychoanalysis

1. Founder of psychoanalysis, originally a therapeutic method of treating neurosis, but in turn developed into a theory of personality, a method of research, and a philosophy of life as well.

2. Developed a systematic, psychological (as opposed to neurological) approach to mental disease.

3. For the first time demonstrated the importance of unconscious and irrational processes in the motivation of human behavior.

4. Opened up for scientific study the area of sexuality and demonstrated its importance as a source of psychological problems, as well as a dynamic in the formation of personality.

5. Focused attention on the importance of early childhood experiences on later personality development and adjustment.

Alfred Adler (1870–1937) — Father of Individual Psychology

1. Eventually broke away from **Freud** in 1911 by emphasizing social factors in personality development and depreciating the importance of the sexual factor.

2. Argued that power, not sexuality, is the basic motive in mental disturbance.

3. Coined the term "life-style" to refer to an individual's characteristic way of expressing his individuality and of reaching his goals.

4. Developed a theory of neurosis which is based primarily on the inferiority complex and the ego defense mechanism of compensation. According to Adler, children experience "inferiority" either in comparison with other children or with adults and occasionally develop an "inferiority complex," which in adulthood may result in neurotic overcompensation

or be used as an excuse for failure.

5. One of the first psychologists to do research on the effects of birth order on personality development.

Otto Rank (1884–1939) — Father of Will Therapy

1. In 1923 began to interpret Freudian concepts in terms of the "birth trauma," i.e., the separation of the child from symbiosis with the mother, the most traumatic experience in the human condition and the root cause of "primal anxiety," which is the basis for all subsequent "separation anxiety." This unorthodox view led to an eventual break with Freud the following year.

2. Developed "will therapy," a short-term therapy consisting of helping the patient to reexperience the birth trauma, and thus anticipated the nontraumatic obstetrical practices of Frédérick Leboyer, the primal therapy of Arthur Janov, and the rebirthing of Leonard Orr.

3. Cofounded the first psychoanalytic journal, *Imago,* in 1912 with H. Sachs (1881–1947).

4. Considered to be one of the great psychologists of art and the artist as reflected in his *Art and Artist* (1909).

C. SWITZERLAND

Eugen Bleuler (1857–1939)

Perhaps best known for his work on dementia praecox, for which he coined and substituted the term "schizophrenia" in 1911.

Carl Jung (1875–1961) — Father of Analytical Psychology

1. Made use of associative reaction time as empirical validation of psychoanalysis, specifically demonstrating the existence of a "complex" or unconscious psychic contents having functional autonomy. This was the first attempt at linking experimental psychology and psychoanalysis.

2. Broke with **Freud** in 1914 because of his depreciation of the importance of sexual libido in personality development.

3. Coined the terms "introvert" and "extrovert" in his

famous work, *Psychological Types* (1921).

4. Introduced the concept of the "collective unconscious," a deposit of archetypes or fundamental modes of apprehension that are common to all humanity.

5. Coined the terms "individuation" and "self-actualization," by which Jung pointed to a process of attaining a healthy, mature, and creative personality.

6. One of the first psychologists to focus on the adult phase of human psychological development and for this reason is sometimes known as the "psychologist of the second half of life," in contrast to Freud, who emphasized early development.

Hermann Rorschach (1882-1922) — Father of Projective Techniques

Developed the famous ink-blot test as early as 1911 but did not publish the test in its present form until 1921. The test, composed of ten cards, was designed to study personality based on the principle of projection, i.e., the individual projects his unconscious motives, etc., onto ambiguous stimuli (ink-blots). The validity of this test has been seriously challenged and equally seriously defended by its users.

D. UNITED STATES

Benjamin Rush (1745-1813) — Father of American Psychiatry

1. Developed the first course in psychiatry in the United States at the University of Pennsylvania in 1791.

2. Wrote the first treatise on psychiatry in America, *Medical Inquiries and Observations upon the Diseases of the Mind* (1812).

3. Influenced by **Pinel,** advocated a more humane treatment of mental patients in America.

Dorothea Dix (1802-1887) — Mother of the Humanitarian Movement for the Insane

Perhaps more than any other individual with the exception of **Pinel,** was responsible for changing the conditions of the existing mental institutions and the founding of new ones in America as well as Europe and even Japan.

Morton Prince (1854–1929) — Father of Abnormal Psychology

1. Best known for treating and recording one of the first case studies on multiple personality, Miss Sally Beauchamp, who manifested as many as five different personalities, described in his popular, *The Dissociation of Personality* (1905).

2. Founded the *Journal of Abnormal Psychology* in 1906.

3. Instrumental in establishing the Harvard Psychological Clinic in 1927, of which he was the first director.

Lightner Witmer (1867–1956) — Father of Clinical Psychology

1. Founded the first psychological clinic at the University of Pennsylvania in 1896, and coined the term "clinical psychology."

2. Founded the first clinical psychological journal, *The Psychological Clinic,* in 1907.

Clifford Beers (1876–1943) — Father of the Mental Hygiene Movement

1. As a result of his description of his mental breakdown and the inhumane treatment he received in mental institutions over a period of three years, summarized in his famous book, *A Mind That Found Itself* (1908), Beers became a leader in what came to be known as the mental hygiene movement.

2. Founded the first Society of Mental Hygiene in Connecticut in 1908, the first National Commission for Mental Hygiene in 1909, and the first International Committee for Mental Hygiene in 1930.

Section II
Innovations

This section contains "firsts" that either are not mentioned in the previous section or are mentioned in passing and deserve emphasis. Those not included in the previous section are presented here because they are the result of efforts by people who are not usually identified with the history of psychology except perhaps for the contribution mentioned herein. Most of these contributions were made in the eighteenth and nineteenth centuries. The order of presentation is chronological after a listing of the so-called "Fathers of Psychology," and the style is question-and-answer format.

Who are the "Fathers of Psychology?"

NAME	FATHER OF
Adler	Individual Psychology
Aristotle	Psychology
Baldwin	Child Psychology*
Beers	Mental Hygiene Movement
Berkeley	Subjective Idealism
Binet	Intelligence Testing

---

*Indicates that the title is shared by two men.

Brentano	Act Psychology
Cattell	Applied Psychology*
Charcot	Neurology
Comte	Positivism
Condillac, de	Sensationalism
Darwin	Evolutionism
Democritus	Materialism
Descartes	Modern Philosophy
Descartes	Physiological Psychology
Dewey	Functional Psychology
Dix	Mother of Humanitarian Movement for the Insane
Epicurus	Epicureanism
Erasistratus	Physiology
Fechner	Psychophysics
Freud	Psychoanalysis
Gall	Phrenology
Galton	Differential Psychology
Galton	Psychometrics
Haeckel	Ecology
Hall	Genetic Psychology
Hall	Adolescent Psychology
Haller, von	Experimental Physiology*
Hartley	British School of Associationism
Herbart	Educational Psychology
Hippocrates	Medicine
Hobbes	Social Psychology
Hume	Modern Skepticism
Husserl	Phenomenology
James	American Psychology
Janet	School of Dissociation
Jung	Analytical Psychology
Kant	Critical Idealism
Kraepelin	Psychopharmacology
Külpe	Würzburg School

---

*Indicates that the title is shared by two men.

Leucippus	Atomism
Locke	British School of Empiricism
Lloyd Morgan	Ethology
McDougall	Hormic (Purposive) Psychology
Mendel	Modern Genetics
Mesmer	Hypnotism
Mill, James	Mental Mechanics
Mill, John	Mental Chemistry
Müller, J.	Experimental Physiology*
Münsterberg	Applied Psychology*
Pavlov	Classical Conditioning
Pinel	Modern Psychiatry
Plotinus	Neo-Platonism
Preyer	Child Psychology*
Prince	Abnormal Psychology
Protagoras	Sophism
Quetelet	Modern Statistics
Rank	Will Therapy
Reid	Scottish School (School of Common Sense)
Romanes	Comparative Psychology
Rorschach	Projective Techniques
Rush	American Psychiatry
Sechenov	Russian Reflexology
Seguin	Special Education
Spearman	Factor Analysis
Stumpf	Psychology of Music
Thales	Philosophy
Thorndike	Instrumental Conditioning
Titchener	Structural Psychology
Watson	Behaviorism
Wertheimer	Gestalt Psychology
Witmer	Clinical Psychology
Wolff, von	Modern Faculty Psychology
Woodworth	Dynamic Psychology

*Indicates that the title is shared by two men.

Wundt   Experimental Psychology
Zeno the Stoic   Stoicism

Who was the first to enunciate a theory of evolution?

1. The first philosopher to articulate the idea of evolution was Anaximandros, a contemporary of **Thales** in the seventh century B.C.

2. Most historians agree that the first modern thinker to work out a theory of organic evolution was Johann Wolfgang von Goethe (1749–1832).

Who was the first to dissect a human cadaver?

Probably **Alcmaeon of Croton,** who lived in the fifth century B.C.

Who was the first to discover the differentiation between the sensory (posterior) and motor (anterior) nerves of the spinal cord?

1. **Erasistratus** (304?–250? B.C.) made the discovery in the third century B.C., but it became lost only to be rediscovered in the nineteenth century.

2. Charles Bell (1774–1842) published his innovative experiment on a rabbit in 1811 demonstrating the differentiation; a Frenchman, François Magendie (1783–1855), came to the same conclusion eleven years later in 1822. A controversy arose as to which investigator should receive credit for the discovery and as a result the principle became known as the Bell-Magendie Law.

Who was the first to use the term psychology?

1. The term "psychologia" was first used by Philip Melanchthon (1497–1560), a collaborator of Martin Luther, in his lectures in Latin on the classics at the University of Wittenberg in Germany.

2. The term first appeared in print in the title of a book in 1590 with the publication of *Psychologia—Hoc Est de*

Hominis Perfectione ("Psychology — This is on the Perfection of Man") by the now forgotten Rudolf Goeckel (1547-1628).

Who was the founder of probability theory as a branch of mathematics?

The credit is usually given to Jacques Bernoulli (1654-1705), whose *Ars conjectandi* ("Art of Wagering") published posthumously in 1713 is considered to be the first systematic presentation of probability theory. This theory was anticipated in the seventeenth century by Blaise Pascal (1623-1662), by Pierre de Fermat (1601-1665) through correspondence in 1654, and by Christian Huygens (1629-1695) in 1657 as "geometry of dice" (*Treatise on Reasoning in Games of Chance*) in response to requests from gamblers to help them with games of chance.

Who was the first to conduct an experiment on sensory differential threshold?

1. Pierre Bouguer (1698-1758) on "illumination" (visual brightness) in 1760 (published posthumously).
2. Charles Delezenne (1776-1866) with his experiment on the differential threshold for the pitch of tones was second in 1827.

Who was the first to demonstrate the electrical nature of nerve energy?

Luigi Galvani (1737-1798) in 1791 when he discovered that electrical current was generated by stimulation of a frog's sciatic nerve.

Who was the first to espouse what came to be known as the "specific energies of nerves," i.e., the differentiation in sensory experience (sight, hearing, etc.) is explained by specific qualities or "energies" of particular nerves as opposed to cortical localization?

The theory was anticipated by Charles Bonnet (1720-1793)

in a document published posthumously in 1797; it was implied in Thomas Young's (1773–1829) theory of color vision in 1802, and Charles Bell (1774–1842) hypothesized that each sense has its own specialized nerve fiber in 1811. However, it remained for **J. Müller** to develop the idea into a full-blown theory as well as christen it in 1826, even though he recognized that cortical localization provided another explanation for the same phenomena.

Who was the first to propose a modern theory of color vision?

Thomas Young (1773–1829) in 1802 when he proposed that there are three types of fibers in the retina that correspond to the three primary colors (red, yellow, and blue) and that respond differentially to light vibrations of different frequencies, producing through combinations all the colors of the visible spectrum. This theory was adopted and clarified in 1852 by **Helmholtz** and became known as the "Young-Helmholtz" theory of color vision, a viable theory to this day.

Who was the first to introduce the concept of "threshold?"

1. The concept of "threshold" was foreshadowed in the atomism of **Democritus** when he stated that nonbodily atoms had to be of a certain strength before they could make an impression on the body and thus be perceived by the sense organ.
2. **Herbart** was the first to postulate the concept of threshold of consciousness to explain forgetting in 1816.

Who was the first to measure "individual differences?"

Friedrich Bessel (1784–1846), a German astronomer, in 1822. Upon reading an article published in 1816 describing the dismissal of Kinnebrook, an assistant at the Greenwich Observatory, by his chief, Maskelyne, because of consistent differences between them in recording times of stellar transits, Bessel developed the concept of the "personal equation," the individual error involved in recording the exact time of an event.

Who was the first to espouse the "trace" theory of memory and forgetting?

Friedrich Beneke (1798–1854) in 1832. The theory was important to the history of psychology because it argued against the belief in the existence of "faculties" in the mind.

Who was the first to systematically use the concept of threshold in physiological experimentation?

Weber, who discovered the "two-point threshold" in the sense of touch in 1834.

Who was the first to argue for cortical localization of specific psychological functions?

1. The belief that the mind has its seat in the brain is quite old and has among its original proponents **Pythagoras** and **Plato,** unlike **Aristotle,** who believed that the seat of the soul is the heart. **Galen** put the matter to rest as far as posterity is concerned, but it remained for **Descartes** to articulate the first theory of how the body and mind interact. **Gall,** the phrenologist, gave the theory a bad name by arguing for more than thirty mental functions localized at various regions in the brain or spots (conformations) on the skull in 1825.

2. The first to offer experimental evidence for cortical localization was Pierre Flourens (1794–1867), who took a more moderate position than **Gall** and argued for a "common action" as well as a "specific action" of different parts of the brain.

3. More impressive evidence for cortical localization was provided by Paul Broca (1824–1880) in 1861, when he performed an autopsy on a man who was afflicted with the loss of memory for words (aphemia) and discovered deterioration in the third convolution of the left frontal lobe where he had predicted it.

4. Finally, the first experiment on direct electrical stimulation of the brain was conducted by Gustav Fritsch (1838–1927) and Eduard Hitzig (1838–1907) in 1870, establishing beyond a doubt the existence of a series of motor centers in the cerebral cortex.

Who taught the first course in experimental psychology?

1. The first course was taught by **Wundt** at the University of Heidelberg in 1867.

2. The first course given in America was taught by **James** at Harvard University in 1875.

What was the first textbook in scientific psychology?

1. The first textbook in any language was the *Grundzüge der physiologischen Psychologie* ("Principles of Physiological Psychology") written by **Wundt** in 1873–1874.

2. Most historians agree that the first text in the English language was the *Outlines of Psychology* written by James Sully (1842–1923) in 1884.

3. A similar textbook was first written in America in 1887 by George T. Ladd (1842–1921) entitled, *Elements of Physiological Psychology*, antedating by three years the classic, *Principles of Psychology*, by **James.**

What was the first psychological journal to be published?

1. The first psychological journal was *Mind*, founded by **Bain** in 1876, although it was somewhat philosophical in orientation.

2. The first journal in experimental psychology was *Philosophische Studien*, founded by **Wundt** in 1881; it ceased publication in 1903.

3. The first psychological journal to be published in America was the *American Journal of Psychology*, founded by **Hall** in 1887 and still extant.

Who founded the first psychological laboratory?

1. Most historians give the credit to **Wundt,** who founded

the psychological laboratory at the University of Leipzig in 1879. The date of its inception has been disputed, although 1879 was the date assigned by Wundt himself, apparently because the first doctoral dissertation was published by Max Friedrich during the 1879–1880 academic year. In fact, there is evidence that Wundt's lab was in operation as early as 1875, the year Wundt came to Leipzig as Professor of Philosophy.

2. The only other laboratory that rivals that of Wundt for priority is the lab founded by **James** at Harvard in 1875 (James was not sure whether it was 1874, 1875, or 1876, and so all three dates are found in the literature.). However, James's lab has been judged too "pocket-sized" (Roback, 1952) to deserve the honor.

The First Psychological Laboratories Throughout the World

COUNTRY	INSTITUTION	FOUNDER	YEAR FOUNDED
Argentina	Buenos Aires	H. G. Pinero	1898
Austria	Graz	A. Meinong	1894
Belgium	Louvain	D. Mercier A. Thiery J. F. Heymans	1891
Canada	Toronto	J. M. Baldwin	1889
Denmark	Copenhagen	A. Lehmann	1886
France	Sorbonne	H. Beaunis A. Binet	1889
Germany	Leipzig	W. Wundt	1879
	Gottingen	G. E. Müller	1881
	Berlin	H. Ebbinghaus	1886
	Munich	C. Stumpf	1889
	Breslau	H. Ebbinghaus	1894
	Würzburg	O. Külpe	1896

Great Britain	Cambridge	W.H.R. Rivers	1897*
	London	W.H.R. Rivers	1897
	Edinburgh	W. G. Smith	1907
	Oxford	W. Brown	1936
Holland	Groningen	G. Heymans	1893
India	Calcutta	N. N. Sengupta	1916
Italy	Inst. of An- thropology (Rome)	G. Sergi	1885
Japan	Tokyo	M. Matsumoto	1903
Poland	Cracow	W. Heinrich	1897
Russia	Kazan	V. Bekhterev	1886
United States	Harvard	W. James	1875
		H. Münsterberg	1892
	Johns Hopkins	G. S. Hall	1883
	Pennsylvania	J. McK. Cattell	1887
	Wisconsin	J. Jastrow	1888
	Indiana	W. L. Bryan	1888
	Clark	G. S. Hall	1889
	Nebraska	H. K. Wolfe	1889
	Michigan	J. H. Tufts	1890
	Columbia	J. McK. Cattell	1891
	Wellesley	M. Calkins	1891
	Catholic	E. A. Pace	1891
	Cornell	F. Angell	1891
	Yale	G. T. Ladd	1892
		E. W. Scripture	
	Brown	E. B. Delabarre	1892
	Princeton	J. M. Baldwin	1893
	Stanford	F. Angell	1893
	Minnesota	J. R. Angell	1893
	Chicago	J. Dewey	1893–94
		J. R. Angell	

*There is some evidence that J. Ward founded a laboratory at Cambridge as early as 1891 but it was more an abortive attempt; also some authorities cite the founding of the Cambridge lab in 1913 when C. S. Myers reestablished the laboratory permanently.

Who was the first American to acquire the Ph.D. in psychology?

1. James McKeen **Cattell** at the University of Leipzig under Wundt in 1886.
2. G. Stanley **Hall** obtained his Ph.D. nominally in psychology from the Department of Philosophy under **James** at Harvard University in 1878 as a kind of afterthought, and thus it is not usually recognized by historians.
3. The first American to obtain his Ph.D. in psychology at an American university was Joseph Jastrow (1863–1944) under **Hall** at Johns Hopkins University also in 1886.

Who established the first psychological clinic?

Witmer at the University of Pennsylvania in 1896.

Who was the first to introduce the maze apparatus into psychological experimentation?

Willard Small (1870–1943) was the first to employ the maze apparatus (modeled on the Hampton Court maze in England) in a study of animal intelligence in 1901.

Who constructed the first intelligence test?

1. The first successful intelligence test was constructed by Théodore Simon (1873–1961) and **Binet** in France in 1905 and successively revised in 1908 and 1911.
2. The first to translate the *Binet-Simon Scale of Intelligence* into English was Henry Goddard (1866–1957) in 1908. However, the *Stanford-Binet,* developed by Lewis Terman (1877–1956) in 1916, became the standard version. The test derived its name from Terman's academic affiliation at Stanford University and became the most widely used individual test of intelligence in the English language until the appearance of the Wechsler tests in the early forties.
3. The first group tests of intelligence were the *Army Alpha* (for English-speaking) and the *Army Beta* (for illiterates and non-English speaking), developed by a group of

psychologists (commissioned by the Army) in 1917 and 1918 respectively, under the directorship of R. M. Yerkes (1876–1956).

Who established the first laboratory for the psychological study of the mentally handicapped?

Henry Goddard (1866–1957) established and became the first director of research at the Vineland (New Jersey) Training School for the Feeble-Minded in 1918.

Who was the first to record the electrical activity of the human brain?

Hans Berger (1873–1943) recorded the electrical nature of the human brain in 1903 and in 1924 developed the electroencephalograph (EEG), using his son as a subject. The findings were published in an article in 1929, in which he described the "alpha rhythm."

Section III
Glossary of Philosophical Terms

This glossary is restricted to those philosophical terms that are frequently omitted in the glossaries of introductory psychology textbooks but are repeatedly used in classroom lectures, much to the chagrin of beginning psychology students. These terms are commonplace in philosophy but not in contemporary psychology; and since there are many students in psychology courses who have no background in philosophy, it is hoped this glossary will begin to meet their need. The glossary also contains extended discussion of major body-mind theories and such important issues as the difference between psychology as a science and philosophy.

ANTHROPOMORPHISM: (G. *anthropos,* man + *morphe,* form) The practice (or tendency) of attributing human characteristics to either superhuman (God) or subhuman (animal) species.

APPERCEPTION: (L. *ad,* to + *percipere,* to perceive) 1. First introduced by **Leibniz** to refer to clear perception, i.e., introspective self-awareness in contradistinction to the unconscious (*"petites perceptions"*) and perception per se (the inner awareness of representations of outer things).

2. Extended by **Kant** to describe the mind's continual organizing of experience in order to achieve unity of perception.

3. Influenced by Kant, **Herbart** used the term to refer to the process by which new experience is affected (transformed) by previous experiences ("apperceptive mass"), for example, the cultivation of taste for a particular food, etc.

4. **Wundt** incorporated all of the above connotations: clear perception, unity of perception, transformation of experience, and argued for the feeling quality of experience as an accompanying end product of apperception.

5. For all its importance in the early history of psychology, the term apperception was virtually abandoned by psychology (in America at least) by the second decade of the twentieth century.

ASSOCIATIONISM: A psychological theory, developed by **Hartley,** following **Aristotle, Hobbes,** and **Locke,** to account for the complexity of experience by reducing mental activity to the sole operations of sensation and association. This position, which has a strong empirical bias, was developed in opposition to the notions of *innate ideas* and mental *faculties* inherent in *rationalism.*

BEHAVIORISM: The psychological school founded by **Watson** which eschewed the validity of such concepts as mind and consciousness and redefined psychology as an objective science of behavior (measurable and observable) from a position of extreme environmentalism in contrast to the *introspectionism* of Wundtian psychology.

BODY-MIND THEORIES: Metaphysical theories concerning the ultimate nature of the body (physiological events) and the mind (mental events) and their interrelationship. The following is a listing of the major body-mind theories according to whether they affirm one (*monism*) or two (*dualism*) principles:

MONISTIC	DUALISTIC
double-aspect theory	hylomorphism
epiphenomenalism	interactionism
hylozoism	parallelism (preestablished
materialism	harmony)
panpsychism	Platonic dualism
psychophysical parallelism	

These theories are defined in the Glossary in their proper alphabetical order.

CAUSALITY: The philosophical characteristic pertaining to the relationship between cause and effect.

CAUSE: (L. *causa,* cause) Something which is both necessary and sufficient to produce an effect. The concept cause is usually distinguished from condition (necessary but not sufficient) and occasion (neither necessary nor sufficient but an encouraging circumstance). For example, hydrogen and oxygen are the causes of water (effect), whereas heat of a certain temperature is a condition and a Bunsen burner in a lab might be an occasion. According to **Aristotle,** four types of causes can be distinguished:
1. material—what a thing is made of.
2. efficient—what sets the process into motion, the agent or force.
3. formal—the pattern or that which gives shape to the substance.
4. final—the purpose or motive for which the agent acts.
For example, the artist (efficient) sculpts the bronze (material) into the shape of a bird (formal) in order to create an ornament for a commission (final).
N.B. In contemporary usage, cause is usually restricted to the efficient cause and occasionally to the final (motive) cause. Material and formal causes are regarded as "characteristics" of the product or effect.

CRITICAL IDEALISM: The epistemological doctrine of **Kant**

that human experience is made possible by 12 *a priori* (transcendental) categories (e.g., unity, causality, existence, etc.) and by the "intuitions" of space and time. What is known is the phenomenon (that which appears), not the noumenon (the thing-in-itself, *Ding-an-sich*), which is unknowable but assumed to exist. Kant attempted a reconciliation of *rationalism* and *empiricism,* trying to prevent the slide of empiricism into the *skepticism* of **Hume.** Also known as transcendental idealism, transcendentalism, German idealism, and Kantianism.

DETERMINISM: The metaphysical doctrine that all phenomena are determined by antecedent causes. The implication in this doctrine is that the relationship between cause and effect is invariant and, therefore, a phenomenon is predictable whenever the relevant causes are known. Sometimes a distinction is made between physical phenomena and psychological phenomena and thus there is physical determinism (*mechanism*), which is attributed to **Democritus** and **Newton,** and psychological determinism (opposite of voluntarism or freedom), which is attributed to **Spinoza.**

DOUBLE-ASPECT THEORY: A body-mind theory that acknowledges the intellectual distinction between mind and body (epistemological *dualism*) but argues that they are simply two "aspects" of some underlying reality, which reduces to a form of (metaphysical) *monism.* Also known as *psychophysical parallelism,* attributed to **Spinoza** (although it was **Fechner** who first used the term), it is probably the most widely held body-mind theory in psychology today, even though the terminology is rarely used and the position is for most implicitly held.

DYNAMIC PSYCHOLOGY: The short-lived school of psychology founded by **Woodworth** in 1918, which strove to achieve an eclectic synthesis of the then existing schools: *functionalism, structuralism,* and *behaviorism.* Because Woodworth was interested in the relationship between the stimulus and the response and saw man as active rather than passive, he termed his synthesis "Dynamic Psychology." This school is not to be confused with psychoanalysis and its derivatives, which are sometimes referred to as "dynamic psychologies."

EMPIRICISM: The epistemological theory that all knowledge is derived through the senses (in opposition to *nativism*) as well as the implication that sense knowledge is more valid than thought or reasoning (in opposition to *rationalism*); attributed to **Locke,** although also found in **Aristotle** (in the first sense), **Bacon,** and **Hobbes.** It is considered a major feature of the scientific method.

EPIPHENOMENALISM: A body-mind theory that consciousness is a mere by-product of the neural processes which underlie it, resulting in the depreciation of concepts like mind, attributed to T. H. Huxley (1825–1895) among others.

EPIPHENOMENON: (G. *epi,* beside + *phenomenon,* that which appears) A by-product or secondary phenomenon that is produced by a primary phenomenon and has no appreciable influence on the primary phenomenon, e.g., fear is an epiphenomenon of trembling according to **James.**

EPISTEMOLOGY: (G. *episteme,* knowledge + *logos,* the study of) The branch of philosophy that studies theories of knowledge, especially its limits and validity.

EUGENICS: (G. *eu,* good, well + *genes,* born) An applied science concerned with improvement of the human race through manipulation of heredity rather than environment (euthenics), founded by **Galton.**

FACULTY: (L. *facultas,* faculty, ability) A formal property or power of the soul hypothesized by medieval philosophers following **Plato** and **Aristotle.** The faculties identified by **Aquinas** were: sensitive, vegetative, locomotive, and rational. Faculty psychology was the resulting study of the mind, focusing on its faculties or powers, an approach that characterized the Middle Ages and was defended by **Wolff** as "rational psychology" in 1734 as superior to "empirical psychology."

FUNCTIONALISM: The psychological point of view that mental processes (e.g., thought, perception, volition, etc.) are adaptive, i.e., functional in the organism's struggle for survival, and that therefore psychology should be interested in the function of mental processes rather than their structure; attributed to **James** and **Dewey.** It eventually became the dominant thrust of the Chicago School, founded by J. R. Angell (1869–1949). This point of view still seems to differentiate American psychology from European psychology, which has a strong *structural* orientation.

GESTALT PSYCHOLOGY: A school of psychology founded by **Wertheimer** in 1912, which originally argued against what was felt to be the reductionism inherent in Wundtian psychology and proposed that the whole pattern or configuration (Gestalt) of behavior including its context ("ground") be studied in addition to analyzing its "contents" (**Wundt**) or elements, since the "whole is greater than the sum of its parts."

HORMIC PSYCHOLOGY: (G. *horme,* purposive striving) A transitional school of psychology founded by **McDougall** in the first decade of the twentieth century that anticipated the shift in American psychology from *functionalism* to *behaviorism* and which argued that man's behavior is primarily motivated by instincts and is therefore purposive or "hormic." Also known as "purposive psychology."

HYLOMORPHISM: (G. *hyle,* matter + *morphe,* form) The body-mind theory that is attributed to **Aristotle** and was championed by **Aquinas,** which states that everything is constituted by two fundamental principles, "prime matter" (pure material potentiality) and "substantial form" (the essence or structure which actualizes the potentiality into the kind of being it is). The example most frequently given is a ball of wax that can take on many different shapes but cannot exist formless; therefore matter cannot exist without some form and vice-versa. For this reason, the theory is considered by some to be a type of *monism.*

HYLOZOISM: (G. *hyle,* matter + *zoe,* life) An ancient body-mind theory, usually restricted to the early Greek philosophers, that life is a property of all matter; therefore it does not distinguish between animate and inanimate.

IDEALISM: The metaphysical doctrine that the world is best conceived of in terms of ideas or thought rather than in terms of matter in space and time (realism).

INNATE IDEAS: A doctrine usually attributed to **Descartes** but originally found in **Plato,** namely that the mind contains notions independent of experience, such as ideas of God, self, perfection, mathematics, etc. **Descartes** vacillated in his conviction about the doctrine and it was apparently not a major part of his system, though it provoked an intellectual revolution in the form of *empiricism.*

INTERACTIONISM: The dualistic body-mind theory proposed by **Descartes** that the mind and body are two separate and independent entities, which can influence each other ("interact") only through the agency of the pineal gland.

INTROSPECTIONISM: (L. *intro,* within + *specere,* to view) The psychological doctrine which characterized Wundtian psychology proposing introspection, an extremely rigorous form of observation of one's own experience that required years of training, as the primary method of psychology and the "contents of consciousness" as its basic data.

ISOMORPHISM: (G. *iso,* same + *morphe,* form) The psychophysical doctrine that there is a topological correspondence (i.e., one in which spatial and temporal orders are preserved but not necessarily in the same magnitude) between fields in the brain and patterns of perception, first articulated by **Lotze**; it eventually became a hallmark of *Gestalt* psychology.

MATERIALISM: The body-mind theory that reduces all reality to a material principle, i.e., matter, implied in **Democritus** and articulated by **Hobbes**. See also *mechanism*.

MECHANISM: The metaphysical doctrine that everything is caused by material, i.e., mechanical, principles, first articulated by **Leucippus** and **Democritus**, an antecedent to *determinism*, the opposite of *vitalism* and *teleology*.

MENTALISM: The epistemological doctrine of **Berkeley** in which he emphasized the subjectivism inherent in Lockean *empiricism*, arguing that our experience is nothing more than a collection of sense impressions and ideas: *"Esse est percipi"* (To be is to be perceived). Berkeley stopped short of *subjective idealism* by positing God, the "Permanent Perceiver," as the guarantor that our sensations are constant and dependable, and positing the soul as the source of the unity of our experience. However, Berkeley's position was quickly detheologized and thus became the foundation stone for *subjective idealism*.

METAPHYSICS: (G. *meta,* beyond, after + *thysis,* physics) The branch of philosophy usually including cosmology (the study of the origin and structure of the universe) and ontology (the study of being). The word acquired its meaning somewhat fortuitously because of the placement of **Aristotle's** works on cosmology and ontology after (*meta*) his works on physics. The adjectival form, metaphysical, is used as described above or sometimes used as a synonym for philosophical as in "metaphysical psychology." The term may also have a pejorative connotation meaning abstract or abstruse.

NAIVE REALISM: The metaphysical position of the so-called man-in-the-street, namely an uncritical (unquestioned) belief in the existence of the external world and the ability to know it, attributed to **Reid** and the Scottish School.

NATIVISM: The epistemological doctrine that the mind has knowledge ("innate ideas"), actually or potentially, which is not derived from experience, attributed to **Descartes** and against which radical *empiricism* argued.

PANPSYCHISM: (G. *pan,* all, everywhere + *psyche,* soul) The body-mind theory that maintains all reality is psychic or pervaded by life, a modern and more sophisticated version of *hylozoism,* attributed to **Fechner.**

PANTHEISM: (G. *pan,* all + *theos,* god) The metaphysical doctrine that equates God with the universe, attributed to **Zeno the Stoic** and **Spinoza.**

PARALLELISM: A dualistic body-mind theory that there is a perfect one-to-one correlation between physical and mental events without any causal relationship between them, created by God to operate in preestablished harmony, as two clocks in perfect synchrony with each other; attributed to **Leibniz.**

PHENOMENALISM: An epistemological theory that knowledge is restricted to phenomena (that which appears) and either denies the existence of the reality (noumenon) behind the phenomenon, as held by **Mach,** or, less frequently, affirms the existence of the noumenon but denies its knowability, e.g., **Kant.**

PHENOMENOLOGY: Though the word has been in use at least since the middle of the eighteenth century by **Kant** and others, **Husserl** was the first to adopt the name to refer to a whole system of philosophy at the beginning of the twentieth century. Husserl defined phenomenology as "a systematic investigation of phenomena, or conscious experiences, especially as they occur immediately in experience without implications."

PHILOSOPHY: (G. *philein,* to love + *sophia,* wisdom) The term is attributed to **Pythagoras** who referred to himself as a "lover of wisdom." Today it is usually defined as a way of knowing that is distinguished from science as follows:

	PHILOSOPHY	SCIENCE
Goal	"truth" understanding (comprehension of the whole)	explanation (determination of causes) control prediction
Reasoning Style	deductive	inductive
Cognitive Style	speculative rationalistic	empirical
Method	introspection appeal to reason	observation hypothesis testing (experimentation)
How?	discursive	rigorous systematic cumulative
What?	"what we would like to know" — B. Russell	"what we can know" — B. Russell
Example	cosmology	astronomy astrophysics

N.B. This is an oversimplified presentation of the differences between philosophy and science but hopefully a useful one nonetheless. The focus is on *metaphysical* philosophy and does not pretend to include all the branches of philosophy such as logic, ethics, and political philosophy. It should also be noted that, somewhat ambiguously, philosophy is sometimes defined as the "science of all things," or "the science of first causes," or even "the science of sciences."

PLATONIC DUALISM: The body-mind theory implicit in the writings of **Plato** that the body and mind (soul) are entirely separate and independent realities; it views the mind as more trustworthy and as, in a sense, a "prisoner of the body."

POSITIVISM: The epistemological position of **Comte,** who argued that knowledge has evolved in three stages: (1) theology, (2) metaphyics (each of which were inadequate), and (3) positivism or the scientific, which limits knowledge to sense data. This notion is important to the history of psychology because it challenged psychology to become a bona fide science in the first half of the nineteenth century.

PRAGMATISM: The philosophical doctrine, first articulated by C. S. Peirce (1839–1914) and espoused by **James** and **Dewey** among others, that the meaning of an idea is best expressed in its practical consequences and that the test of the truth of an idea or belief is the degree to which it works; "Truth is what works" (Dewey).

PSYCHOLOGY: (G. *psyche,* breath, spirit, soul, mind + *logos,* word, the study of) Originally, psychology meant the study of the soul, the principle of life, and all of its properties. Gradually, the term came to mean the study of the mind, and more recently, the scientific study of experience (Wundt) or of behavior (Watson).

PSYCHIATRY: (G. *psyche,* soul + *iatri,* to heal) Branch of medicine that attempts to treat, diagnose, and prevent mental, emotional, and behavioral disorders.

PSYCHOPHYSICAL PARALLELISM: Cf. double-aspect theory.

RATIONALISM: (L. *ratio,* reason) The epistemological theory that by pure reasoning, without appeal to any empirical data, we can arrive at substantive knowledge about the world. Spawned by **Plato,** the three greatest rationalists were **Descartes, Spinoza,** and **Leibniz.**

REALISM: The metaphysical doctrine that physical objects exist independent of experience. Epistemologically, realism holds that the senses are accurate and that it is possible to have a true and direct knowledge of the world.

REFLEXOLOGY: A psychological viewpoint first attributed to the Russian, **Sechenov,** contending that all behavior, both voluntary and involuntary, can be explained in terms of reflexes and that the study of behavior is adequate for an understanding of all psychology.

SCIENCE: (L. *scire,* to know) Refers to both the process and the product of a highly refined way of knowing. Science has been defined as the intentional experience of error (experimentation) by some and "snooping around full-time" by others. Cf. discussion at *philosophy.*

SENSATIONALISM: An extreme version of empiricism which maintains that all knowledge is ultimately derived from experience and all experience from sensation, the antithesis of *rationalism,* attributed to **de Condillac** among others. Also known as sensationism.

SKEPTICISM: (G. *skeptesthai,* to look, consider) The epistemological doctrine concerning the limits of knowledge, namely that "true" knowledge is unobtainable or, at least, unrecognizable, attributed to **Hume.**

SOLIPSISM: (L. *solus,* alone + *ipse,* self) The metaphysical view that the individual self is the whole of reality and therefore only one's own experience can be known; counterpart to *skepticism,* attributed to **Hume.**

STRUCTURALISM: The psychological viewpoint that became formalized into a school of psychology identified with **Titchener** that defined psychology as the study of the contents (structure) of consciousness from the point of view of the experiencer via the method of introspection, a rigorous simplification of Wundtian psychology. Usually contrasted with *functionalism*.

SUBJECTIVE IDEALISM: The epistemological doctrine that one's (mental) experience is the only knowable reality, attributed to **Berkeley**. Cf. *mentalism*.

TELEOLOGY: The metaphysical doctrine that purpose or design is immanent (inherent) in nature, emphasizing the future rather than the past and therefore in contrast to *determinism*, attributed to **Aristotle.**

VITALISM: (L. *vita,* life) The biological-philosophical doctrine that life possesses a vital principle ("entelechy") that is not reducible to physico-chemical forces, opposite of *materialism,* attributed to Georg E. Stahl (1666–1734) and popularized by **J. Müller.**

Section IV
Classics in the History of Psychology

Annotated list of the seminal works that contributed to the historical development of psychology as a science from c. 400 B.C. to the 1930s. The title given is the English translation unless the work has never been translated; then the original title is given.

B.C.

c. 400   *On the sacred disease.*   Hippocrates
           (Epilepsy is an organic, not
           "sacred," disease)

c. 400   *Nature of man.*   Hippocrates
           (Theory of four humors to
           explain illness)

c. 390–348 *Dialogues.* (Esp. *Phaedo,*   Plato
           Phaedrus, and *Timaeus*)
           (Affirms the immortality of the
           soul)

c. 390–348 *Republic.*   Plato

(The first Utopia; the allegory
of the cave)

c. 350   *On the soul.*   Aristotle
              (First systematic discussion of
              the soul and first history of
              psychology)

c. 300   *Characters.*   Theophrastus
              (First treatise on psychological
              typology)

A.D.
c. 200   *On the natural faculties.*   Galen
              (Formulation of first theory of
              personality based on Hippo-
              crates' four humors)

c. 400   *The confessions.*   St. Augustine
              (First psychological
              autobiography)

1269–1270 *On the soul.*   Aquinas
              (First systematic treatise on
              faculty psychology)

1575   *The tryal of wits.*   Huarte
              (First treatise on differential
              psychology)

1590   *Psychology—This is on the*   Goeckel
              perfection of man.
              (First time the word "psychology"
              appears in print)

1620   *The new organon of the sciences.*   Bacon
              (Formal declaration of
              independence of man's thinking
              from metaphysics and deduction—
              the empirical manifesto)

1637   *Discourse on the method of*   Descartes

rightly conducting the reason.
(The beginning of modern
philosophy, contains the famous
"Cogito, ergo sum.")

| 1649 | *The passions of the soul.*
(One of the first psychological
theories of the emotions; contains
the theory of interactionism) | Descartes |

| 1650 | *Human nature: Or the*
fundamental elements of policy.
(Consciousness is reduced to an
epiphenomenon) | Hobbes |

| 1651 | *Leviathon or, the matter, form,*
and power of commonwealth,
ecclesiastical and civil.
(First treatise on social psychology) | Hobbes |

| 1657 | *Treatise on reasoning in games*
of chance.
(First treatise on probability
theory) | Huygens |

| 1662 | *Treatise on man.*
(First textbook on physiology) | Descartes |

| 1687 | *Mathematical principles of natural*
philosophy.
(First articulation of scientific
determinism) | Newton |

| 1690 | *Essay concerning human*
understanding.
(Establishment of British
Empiricism; *tabula rasa;* primary
and secondary qualities;
association of ideas) | Locke |

1709	*As essay toward a new theory of vision.* (First psychological monograph)	Berkeley
1710	*A treatise concerning the principles of human knowledge.* (Foundation of subjective idealism)	Berkeley
1713	*Art of wagering.* (First systematic presentation of probability theory)	Bernoulli
1732	*Empirical psychology.*	von Wolff
1734	*Rational psychology.* (First to distinguish between "empirical" and "rational" psychology; systematic treatment of faculty psychology)	von Wolff
1739–1740	*A treatise of human nature.* (Foundation of skepticism and solipsism; causality is explained as habit of mind)	Hume
1749	*Observations on man.* (Establishment of British School of Associationism; provided associationism with a physiological basis)	Hartley
1754	*Treatise on the sensations.* (Establishment of sensationalism, an extreme version of Locke's empiricism; contains the famous illustration of the sentient statue)	de Condillac
1760	*On the differential threshold for illumination.* (Contains the first experiment on sensory differential threshold, on visual brightness)	Bouguer

| 1779 | *Memoir on the discovery of animal magnetism.* (First treatise in the West on hypnosis, originally called "animal magnetism" or mesmerism) | Mesmer |

| 1781 | *Critique of pure reason.* (Establishment of critical idealism; considered to be one of the greatest works of modern philosophy) | Kant |

| 1791 | *Commentary on effects of electricity on muscular motion.* (First demonstration of the electrical nature of nerve energy, in opposition to the "animal spirits" of Descartes) | Galvani |

| 1796 | *Analyse abregée de l'essai analytique.* (The first suggestion of the "specific energies of nerves" theory, which anticipated J. Müller's [1826] elaborate presentation by 30 years) | Bonnet |

| 1801 | *A treatise on insanity.* (Empirical view of mental illness; contains a plea for more humane treatment of mental patients) | Pinel |

| 1801 | *The wild boy of Aveyron.* (One of first scientifically recorded case studies of a so-called "feral child" and the attempt to civilize him) | Itard |

| 1802 | "On the theory of light and colours" | Young |

(First presentation of a modern theory of color vision, with a heavy debt to Newton, that would eventually become the "Young-Helmholtz" theory 50 years later)

1809   *Researches on the nervous system.*   Gall & Spurzheim
(Establishment of phrenology)

1809   *Zoological philosophy.*   Lamarck
(First presentation of the doctrine of the inheritance of acquired characteristics)

1811   *Idea of a new anatomy of the brain.*   Bell
(The first experiment — on a rabbit — that differentiated between the sensory [posterior] and motor [anterior] nerves of the spinal cord)

1812   *Medical inquiries and observations upon the diseases of the mind.*   Rush
(First treatise on psychiatry by an American)

1816   *A text-book in psychology: An attempt to found the science of psychology on experience, metaphysics, and mathematics.*   Herbart
(Textbook in psychology representing the last great system of metaphysical psychology)

1820   *Lectures on the philosophy of the human mind.*   Brown
(First articulation of the nine

secondary laws of association)

1822	"Experiments upon the functions of the roots of the spinal nerves" (A sequel to Bell's [1811] report on the differentiation of nerves in the spinal cord which eventually led to the so-called Bell-Magendie Law)	Magendie
1822–1823	*Astronomical observations in Königsberg* (The recorded account of the "personal equation," which led to research on the differential threshold)	Bessel
1824	*Experimental researches on the properties and the functions of the nervous system in vertebrate animals.* (First to offer experimental evidence for cortical localization of the brain, arguing for "common action" as well as "specific action" of different parts of the brain)	Flourens
1826	"On the nervous circle which connects the voluntary muscles with the brain" (Contains the first reference to the "sixth sense," today known as kinesthesia)	Bell
1827	"On the differential threshold for the pitch of tone" (The second experiment on sensory differential threshold, following Bouguer [1760])	Delezenne

| 1829 | *Analysis of the phenomena of the human mind.* (Radical associationism, "mental mechanics") | Mill, James |

| 1830–1842 | *Introduction to positive philosophy.* (Establishment of positivism, which challenged psychology to become a bona fide science) | Comte |

| 1832 | *A textbook of psychology as a natural science.* (Contains the first articulation of "trace" theory to explain memory and forgetting) | Beneke |

| 1833–1840 | *Elements of human physiology.* (First great textbook of physiology; contains doctrine of "specific energies of nerves") | Müller, J. |

| 1834 | *De pulsu, resorptione, auditu, et tactu: Annotationes anatomicae et physiologicae.* (The first systematic use of the concept of threshold in psychological experimentation) | Weber |

| 1835 | *A treatise on man and the development of his faculties.* (First treatise on modern statistics) | Quetelet |

| 1843 | *System of logic, ratiocinative and inductive, being a connected view of the principles of evidence, and the methods of scientific investigation.* (First systematic presentation of the "canons" of experimental | Mill, J. S. |

inquiry: agreement, difference, joint method, concomitant variations, and residues)

1846	*On the sense of touch and common sensibility.* (Although Weber published his findings in an earlier paper in 1834, this is the standard reference to the "just noticeable difference" threshold as well as what came to be known as "Weber's Law")	Weber
1850	"On the rate of transmission of nerve impulse" (First attempt to measure the speed of conduction of the nerve impulse)	Helmholtz
1852	*Medizinische Psychologie oder Physiologie der Seele.* (Contains the famous "local signs" theory of visual space perception as well as the first articulation of psychological isomorphism)	Lotze
1855	*The senses and the intellect.*	Bain
1859	*The emotions and the will.* (Considered to be *the* textbooks in psychology in the English language for almost 50 years before the establishment of Wundtian psychology)	Bain
1856–1866	*Treatise on physiological optics.* (Classic on vision, sensation, and perception, including the Young-Helmholtz theory of color vision)	Helmholtz

1859	*Origin of the species.* (First to supply empirically persuasive evidence for a theory of evolution)	Darwin
1860	*Elements of psychophysics.* (First articulation of psychophysics, in which various methods of psychophysical measurement are set forth as well as "Fechner's Law")	Fechner
1861	"Remarques sur le siège de la faculté du langage articulé, suivies d'une observation d'aphémie (perte de la parole)." (One of the first accounts to offer experimental evidence in support of cortical localization of specific psychological functions — in this case, aphemia, i.e., loss of memory for words)	Broca
1863	*On the sensations of tone.* (First articulation of the "resonance" theory of audition)	Helmholtz
1863	*Reflexes of the brain.* (First articulation of what came to be known as "reflexology," anticipating behaviorism)	Sechenov
1865	"On the rapidity of the thought and of the determination of the will." (First realization of the significance of reaction time as a way of measuring psychological processes, which came to be known as "mental chronometry")	Donders

1865	*Experiments in plant hybridization.* (First articulation of modern genetic theory of trait transmission, which came to be known as "Mendel's Law")	Mendel
1869	*Hereditary genius.* (First modern treatise on differential psychology; established the case for eugenics)	Galton
1870	"Ueber die elektrische Erregbarkeit des Grosshirns" (The first experiment on direct electrical stimulation of a brain)	Fritsch & Hitzig
1871	*Descent of man.* (Darwin extends the theory of evolution to include man)	Darwin
1872	*Expressions of emotions in man and animals.* (Presents one of the first scientific theories of the emotions)	Darwin
1872–1875	*Zur Lehre vom Lichtsinne.* (Articulation of famous theory of color vision that rivaled the Young-Helmholtz theory)	Hering
1873–1874	*Principles of physiological psychology.* (First great textbook in experimental psychology)	Wundt
1874	*Psychology from an empirical standpoint.* (Presentation of "act psychology," which served as a	Brentano

counterpoint to the structuralism
of Wundtian psychology)

| 1877 | *Biographical sketch of an infant.* (First "baby biography") | Darwin |

| 1881 | *The mind of the child.* (The first textbook in child psychology) | Preyer |

| 1882 | *Animal intelligence.* (First textbook on comparative psychology) | Romanes |

| 1883 | *Compendium of psychiatry.* (A nosology of mental disorders that provided the basis for much of present-day psychiatric nomenclature) | Kraepelin |

| 1883–1890 | *Tonpsychologie.* (First book on the psychology of music) | Stumpf |

| 1884 | *Outlines of psychology.* (First textbook in scientific psychology in the English language) | Sully |

| 1885 | *Memory: A contribution to experimental psychology.* (First systematic experimental investigation of learning and forgetting) | Ebbinghaus |

| 1886 | "Psychology" (Famous article that first appeared in the ninth edition of the *Encyclopaedia Britannica* arguing for a dynamic conception of the mind against associationism) | Ward |

1887	*Elements of physiological psychology.* (First textbook in scientific psychology published in America)	Ladd
1890	*Principles of psychology.* (Still considered one of the greatest textbooks in psychology ever written)	James
1890	"On the form quality" (First presentation of the concept of a "form quality" of an object that transcends mere sensations, as in the melody of a song; anticipated the Gestalt movement)	Ehrenfels
1893–1912	*Mathematical contributions to the theory of evolution.* (Introduced for the first time the formulas in use today for standard deviation, correlation coefficient [Pearson], and chi square)	Pearson
1894	*An introduction to comparative psychology.* (Argued against the anthropomorphic approach to the study of animals and articulated the law of parsimony or "Lloyd Morgan's Canon")	Lloyd Morgan
1895	*Mental development in the child and the race.* (Classic on child psychology from the ontogenetic viewpoint)	Baldwin
1896	"The reflex arc concept in psychology" (Considered to be the	Dewey

functionalist manifesto)

1900	*The interpretation of dreams.* (The work that established Freud as a major thinker and probably his most important work)	Freud
1901	"Experimental study of the mental processes of the rat, II" (The first to employ the maze apparatus in a psychological experiment)	Small
1901	"The influence of improvement in one mental function upon the other functions" (Classic experiment on "transfer of training")	Woodworth & Thorndike
1901–1905	*Experimental psychology.* (Considered one of the most astute laboratory manuals ever written in the English language by Külpe among others)	Titchener
1902	*Varieties of religious experience.* (Classic in the area of the psychology of religion; gave respectability to the topic)	James
1903	*Educational psychology.* (First textbook in the field of educational psychology)	Thorndike
1904	*On conditioned reflexes.* (The first public reference to the "conditioned reflex" on the occasion of his acceptance of the Nobel Prize for physiology in 1904)	Pavlov
1904	*Adolescence: Its psychology and*	Hall

*its relations to physiology,
anthropology, sociology, sex,
crime, religion and education.*
(First textbook on the psychology
of adolescence)

1905	*The dissociation of a personality.* (The first published case study of multiple personality)	Prince
1908	*Introduction to social psychology.* (First textbook in the field of social psychology; one of the all- time best sellers in psychology and still in print)	McDougall
1908	*The mind that found itself.* (The book that started the mental hygiene movement)	Beers
1911	*Dementia praecox, or the group of schizophrenias.* (First text to use the term "schizophrenia"; considered to be a landmark work on the illness)	Bleuler
1912	*The psychological methods of testing intelligence.* (The first presentation of the "mental quotient," which provided a technique for making the "mental age" of Binet more meaningful by dividing it by the chronological age; all that remained was multiplying it by 100 to generate the "intelligence quotient," which Terman suggested in 1916)	Stern
1912	"Experimentelle Studien über das Sehen von Bewegung"	Wertheimer

(A monograph on "apparent movement" or the phi phenomenon, which was the beginning of Gestalt psychology)

1913	"Psychology as the behaviorist views it." (The behaviorist manifesto)	Watson
1915	"Contents of children's minds." (The study that began the child-study movement)	Hall
1917	*The mentality of apes.* (As a result of experiments with apes on the Teneriffe Islands, Köhler argued against the "trial and error" theory of Thorndike as the sole explanation of animal learning and posited "insight" learning as an alternative)	Köhler
1918	*Dynamic psychology.* (An attempt to integrate structuralism and behaviorism into a functionalist framework)	Woodworth
1921	*Psychological types.* (Introduced the distinction between introversion and extroversion; perhaps Jung's best-known work)	Jung
1921	*Psychodiagnostics: A diagnostic test based on perception.* (The first and most famous of all projective tests, comprised of ten ink-blots)	Rorschach
1922	*Senescence: the last half of life.* (The first book on the psychology of aging)	Hall

| 1923 | *The trauma of birth.* (The first of a long tradition of therapists who view the birth trauma as the root of anxiety) | Rank |

| 1927 | *The abilities of man.* (The first presentation of the two-factor theory of intelligence) | Spearman |

| 1928 | *Psychological care of the infant and child.* (First book on child-rearing written by a psychologist) | Watson |

| 1929 | "On the electroencephalogram of men" (The first successful recording [EEG] of the electrical activity of the brain) | Berger |

| 1935 | *The principles of Gestalt psychology.* (Considered one of the best syntheses of Gestalt psychology) | Koffka |

Section V
Annotated Bibliographic Guide to Secondary Sources

The following is a comprehensive list of secondary sources in the history of psychology. Not all of the books are currently in print, but they are included here because of their importance and should be available at most university libraries. With time, publishers and editions change and so the reader is referred to *Books in Print* for the most up-to-date information. The second date in parenthesis at the end of the entry is the publication date of the first edition where applicable.

I. General

Boring, E. G. *A history of experimental psychology.* (2nd ed.) New York: Appleton-Century-Crofts, 1950. (1929)
(The most complete and scholarly history of modern psychology in the English language, "the bible"; indispensable for the serious student)

Brennan, R. E. *History of psychology: From the standpoint of a Thomist.* New York: Macmillan, 1945.

(An excellent brief history of psychology, with the interesting bias of a Thomistic philosopher)

Brett, G. S. *Brett's history of psychology.* (Edited and abridged by R. S. Peters) New York: Macmillan, 1953. (1912–1921)

(A successful abridgement of one of the first and still one of the best accounts in English of the "long past" of psychology)

Esper, E. A. *A history of psychology.* Philadelphia: Saunders, 1964.

(A scholarly text with the majority of the book covering the ancient Greek philosphers through Aristotle)

Faucher, R. E. *Pioneers of psychology.* New York: Norton, 1979.

(A history of psychology using the biographical approach, beginning with Descartes through Piaget and Skinner)

Leahey, T. H. *A history of psychology.* Englewood Cliffs, N.J.: Prentice-Hall, 1980.

(Covers much the same ground as Brett [1953] but in a more contemporary style aimed at today's undergraduate and from an acknowledged "rationalist" point of view)

Lowry, R. *The evolution of psychological theory: 1650 to the present.* Chicago: Aldine, 1971.

(A brief, conceptual history of psychology within a theoretical framework from the beginning of the modern period [Descartes] up to the era of schools)

MacLeod, R. B. *The persistent problems of psychology.* Pittsburgh, Pa.: Duquesne University Press, 1975.

(An incomplete account of the "persistent" philosophical problems in the history of psychology from a phenomenological point of view)

Miller, G. A. *Psychology: The science of mental life.* New York: Harper & Row, 1962.

(A personalized version of the significant events in the history of psychology, originally intended as a series of lectures for undergraduate students in the introductory course at Harvard)

Misiak, H. *The philosophical roots of scientific psychology*. New York: Fordham University Press, 1961.
(The title says it all)

Misiak, H., and Sexton, V. S. *History of psychology:An overview*. New York: Grune & Stratton, 1966.
(A schematic presentation of the history of psychology from its earliest philosophical roots to some of its most recent manifestations)

Misiak, H., and Staudt, V. M. *Catholics in psychology: A historical overview*. New York: McGraw-Hill, 1954.
(Biographical coverage of individuals sufficiently ignored in the standard textbooks to merit separate treatment, beginning with Cardinal Mercier [1851-1926])

Müller-Freienfels, R. *The evolution of modern psychology*. (Translated by W. B. Wolfe) New Haven, Conn.: Yale University Press, 1935.
(Interesting to American readers because of its European point of view, which seems to be more at home with philosophy)

Murphy, G., and Kovach, J. K. *Historical introduction to modern psychology*. (3rd ed.) New York: Harcourt Brace Jovanovich, 1972. (1949)
(Covers essentially the same ground as Boring [1950] but written for the undergraduate student and brought up to the present with extensive thematic chapters)

Roback, A. A. *History of psychology and psychiatry*. New York: Philosophical Library, 1961.
(Brief sketches of some 150 outstanding contributors to the history of psychology and psychiatry)

Robinson, D. N. *An intellectual history of psychology*. New York: Macmillan, 1976.
(A history of psychology presented as a history of ideas that challenges contemporary psychology's physiological

and behavioristic biases)

Sahakian, W. S. *History and systems of psychology.* New York: Halsted Press, 1975.
(Written from the schools approach, not only as schools of thought, but with particular emphasis on university centers as spheres of influence)

Schultz, D. P. *A history of modern psychology.* (2nd ed.) New York: Academic Press, 1975. (1969)
(A recent text that concentrates on the last century of psychology as a science and "written expressly for the undergraduate student's initial exposure to the history of his discipline, and not the instructor teaching the course")

Watson, R. I. *The great psychologists.* (4th ed.) Philadelphia: Lippincott, 1978. (1963)
(Using the biographical approach: six chapters are devoted to ancient and medieval thinkers; three to early modern philosophers who helped to mold modern psychology; eleven to those who shaped modern psychology beginning with Fechner through Freud; with two final chapters discussing recent developments in Europe and the U.S.)

Wertheimer, M. *A brief history of psychology.* New York: Holt, Rinehart & Winston, 1970.
(The title captures its essence)

Zilboorg, G., and Henry, G. W. *A history of medical psychology.* New York: Norton, 1941.
(Remains the classic in the history of psychiatry and clinical psychology from ancient times to Freud and his contemporaries in the twentieth century, written from a decidedly psychoanalytic point of view)

Zusne, L. *Names in the history of psychology.* Washington, D.C.: Hemisphere Publishing Corporation, 1975.
(A sourcebook of 526 biographical entries arranged in chronological order from Heraclitus to Hovland [d. 1961])

II. American

Roback, A. A. *A history of American psychology.* (Rev. ed.)

New York: Collier, 1964. (1952)
(The only one and indeed a very good one, although somewhat idiosyncratic)

III. Systematic

Chaplin, J. and Krawiec, T. S. *Systems and theories in psychology.* (3rd ed.) New York: Holt, Rinehart & Winston, 1974. (1960)
(History of psychology from the systematic, i.e., topical, point of view, including all the traditional categories: sensation, perception, learning, thinking, motivation, feeling and emotion, physiology, quantitative, and personality)

Heidbreder, E. *Seven psychologies.* New York: Appleton-Century-Crofts, 1933.
(An astute and sober account of the main psychological movements judged significant in the early 1930s: structuralism, Jamesian psychology, functionalism, behaviorism, dynamic psychology, Gestalt psychology, and psychoanalysis)

Krantz, D. L. (Ed.) *Schools of psychology: A symposium.* New York: Appleton-Century-Crofts, 1969.
(A retrospective evaluation of the schools covered in Heidbreder's [1933] book, written by specialists)

Marx, M. H., and Hillix, W. A. *Systems and theories in psychology.* (2nd ed.) New York: McGraw-Hill, 1973. (1963)
(Combines the school approach of Heidbreder [1933] in the first half with the systems approach of Chaplin & Krawiec [1974] in the second half)

Misiak, H., and Sexton, V. S. *Phenomenological, existential, and humanistic psychologies: A historical survey.* New York: Grune & Stratton, 1973.
(Perhaps the best history available of what has come to be known as the "Third Force" in psychology today, tracing the development from the philosophy of Husserl to the psychology of Maslow)

Spiegelberg, H. *The pheneomenological movement: A histor-*

ical introduction. (2nd ed.) (2 vols.) The Hague: Nijhoff, 1965. (1960)

(The authoritative history of the development of phenomenology from its inception with Brentano up to Sartre and Merleau-Ponty and their American contemporaries)

Spiegelberg, H. *Phenomenology in psychology and psychiatry: A historical introduction.* Evanston, Ill.: Northwestern University Press, 1972.

(Covers much the same ground as Misiak & Sexton [1973] but with a much heavier emphasis on European figures)

Wann, T. W. (Ed.) *Behaviorism and phenomenology: Contrasting bases for modern psychology.* Chicago: University of Chicago Press, 1964.

(An animated confrontation between behaviorism defended by Skinner against the attacks of humanistic psychologists such as Rogers and others)

Wolman, B. B. *Contemporary theories and systems in psychology.* New York: Harper & Row, 1960.

(A comprehensive overview of contemporary psychological theory)

Woodworth, R. S., & Sheehan, M. R. *Contemporary schools of psychology.* (3rd ed.) New York: Ronald Press, 1964. (1931)

(A classic text on the schools that rivaled Heidbreder's [1933] book but is more contemporary because of its revisions)

IV. Readings

Dennis, W. (Ed.) *Readings in the history of psychology.* New York: Appleton-Century-Crofts, 1948.

(Sixty-one selections from Aristotle [c. 330 B.C.] on memory and recollection to Hull [1930] on trial and error learning, with over half the selections published since 1850)

Herrnstein, R. J., & Boring , E. G. (Eds.) *A source book in the history of psychology*. Cambridge, Mass.: Harvard University Press, 1965.
(One hundred and sixteen selections from Aristotle [c. 350 B.C.] on the five senses to Lashley [1929] on cerebral equipotentiality and mass action, organized under 15 topics with illuminating introductions and commentaries)

Sahakian, W. S. (Ed.) *History of psychology: A source book in systematic psychology*. Itasca, Ill.: F. E. Peacock, 1968.
(Two hundred and four selections from 133 contributors beginning with Plato [c. 390–348 B.C.] to Maslow [1962], organized into 26 categories)

Watson, R. I. (Ed.) *Basic writings in the history of psychology*. New York: Oxford University Press, 1979.
(Forty-eight selections from the modern period beginning with Galileo [1623] to Skinner [1971], with extensive commentary)

V. Dictionaries

Baldwin, J. M. (Ed.) *Dictionary of philosophy and psychology*. New York: Macmillan, 1901.
(Comprehensive and authoritative for its time; approximately 75 collaborators from all over the world; a classic primarily of historical interest)

Drever, J. *A dictionary of psychology*. Rev. ed. by H. Wallerstein. Baltimore, Md.: Penguin Books, 1964. (1952)
(An inexpensive, paperbound, pocket-sized dictionary that was prepared by a Scotsman who "made a speciality of explaining the difficult concepts of psychology in easy terms" and succeeded)

English, H. B., and English, A. *A comprehensive dictionary of psychological and psychoanalytical terms: A guide to usage*. New York: McKay, 1958.
(Although somewhat dated, still considered to be the best and most comprehensive dictionary of psychology in the English language)

Harriman, P. L. *Handbook of psychological terms*. Totowa,
   N.J.: Littlefield, Adams, 1965. (1959)
   (An inexpensive, paperbound dictionary with brief defini-
   tions geared to the undergraduate)

Runes, D. D. (Ed.) *Dictionary of philosophy*. Totowa, N.J.:
   Littlefield, Adams, 1962. (1960)
   (An inexpensive, paperbound dictionary of philosophy
   comprised of definitions written by 72 authorities who
   have signed their entries; the best dictionary of philosophy
   I know of)

Warren, H. C. *Dictionary of psychology*. Boston: Houghton
   Mifflin, 1934.
   (A classic which remained the best of its kind until
   superseded by English & English [1958]; it still has
   historical value although out of print)

VI. Bibliography

Watson, R. I. (Ed.) *Eminent contributors to psychology*. (2
   vols.) New York: Springer, 1974, 1976.
   (Vol. 1 contains more than 12,000 primary references for
   538 eminent contributors to psychology who lived between
   1600 and 1967; vol. 2 contains more than 50,000 secondary
   references for 530 of the 538 eminent contributors)

VII. Autobiographies

(The following citations refer to two ongoing series of
autobiographical sketches of the more recent eminent men
and women in the field since 1930, only a few of whom are
mentioned in this *Guide*. The contributors to each volume are
listed for those who wish more information.)

Murchison, C. A. (Ed.) *A history of psychology in autobiography*. Worcester, MA.: Clark University Press, 1930–
   1936.

Volume I	Volume II	Volume III
1930	1932	1936
J. M. Baldwin	B. Bourdon	J. R. Angell
M. W. Calkins	J. Drever	F. C. Bartlett
E. Claparede	K. Dunlap	M. Bentley
R. Dodge	G. C. Ferrari	H. A. Carr
P. Janet	S. I. Frank	S. DeSanctis
J. Jastrow	K. Groos	J. Froebes
F. Kiesow	G. Heymans	O. Klemm
W. McDougall	H. Hoffding	K. Marbe
C. E. Seashore	C. H. Judd	C. S. Myers
W. Stern	W. B. Pillsbury	E. L. Thorndike
C. Stumpf	L. M. Terman	J. B. Watson
H. C. Warren	M. F. Washburn	W. Wirth
T. Ziehen	R. S. Woodworth	
H. Zwaardemaker	R. M. Yerkes	

Boring, E. G., Langfeld, H. S., Werner, H., and Yerkes, R. M. (Eds.) *A history of psychology in autobiography*. (Vol. IV) Worcester, MA.: Clark University Press, 1952. (W.V.D. Bingham; E. G. Boring; C. L. Burt; R. M. Elliott; A. Gemelli; A. Gesell; C. L. Hull; W. S. Hunter; D. Katz; A. Michotte; J. Piaget; H. Pieron; C. Thomson; L. L. Thurstone; E. C. Tolman)

Boring, E. G., and Lindzey, G. (Eds.) *A history of psychology in autobiography*. (Vol. V) New York: Appleton-Century-Crofts, 1967. (G. W. Allport; L. Carmichael; K. M. Dallenbach; J. F. Dashiell; J. J. Gibson; K. Goldstein; H. Helson; W. R. Miles; G. Murphy; H. A. Murray; S. L. Pressey; C. R. Rogers; B. F. Skinner; M. S. Viteles)

Lindzey, G. (Ed.) *A history of psychology in autobiography*. (Vol. VI) Englewood Cliffs, New Jersey: Prentice-Hall, 1974. (F. H. Allport; F. A. Beach; R. B. Cattell; C. H. Graham; E. R. Hilgard; O. Klineberg; J. Konorski; D. Krech; A. R.

Luria; M. Mead; O. H. Mowrer; T. M. Newcomb; S. S. Stevens)

Lindzey, G. (Ed.) *A history of psychology in autobiography.* (Vol. VII) San Francisco: W. H. Freeman, 1980.
(A. Anastasi; D. E. Broadbent; J. S. Bruner; H. J. Eysenck; F. A. Geldard; E. J. Gibson; D. O. Hebb; Q. McNemar; C. E. Osgood; R. R. Sears; H. A. Simon)

Krawiec, T. S. (Ed.) *The psychologists.* (Vols. I & II) New York: Oxford University Press, 1972, 1974.

Volume I 1972	Volume II 1974
A. Anastasi	H. L. Ansbacher
I. A. Berg	J. Brožek
W. R. Garner	R. B. Cattell
H. Helson	J. M. Hunt
W. A. Hunt	A. R. Jensen
J. Kagan	H. H. Kendler
W. J. McKeachie	R. W. Leeper
M. B. Smith	G. Murphy
F. C. Thorne	C. E. Osgood
R. I. Watson	C. Pfaffmann
W. B. Webb	M. S. Viteles
P. T. Young	

Index of Names

(Page numbers in **boldface** type indicate the pages on which there is major discussion.)

105

Index of Subjects

Abnormal psychology, 50, 53
Acquired characteristics, inheritance of, 22, 82
Act psychology, 30, 32, 52, 87
Adolescent psychology, 39, 52, 91
American psychiatry, 49, 53
American Psychological Association, 39, 40
American psychology, 38, 52
Analytical psychology, 48, 52
Animal magnetism, 46, 81
Anthropomorphism, 36, 63, 89
Anxiety, 48, 93
Apparent movement, 33, 92
Apperception, 17, 21, 30, 63–64
Apperceptive mass, 24, 64
Applied psychology, 40, 41, 52, 53
Association, laws of, 24, 41, 79, 82–83
Associationism, 8, 15, 19, 20, 24, 43, 52, 64, 80, 84, 88
Archetypes, 49
Atomism, 5, 6, 53

Baby biography, 23, 88
Behavior, 42, 43, 73
Behaviorism, 29, 34, 38, 41, 42, 43, 53, 64, 66, 68, 86, 92
Bell-Magendie Law, 54, 83
Birth trauma, 48, 93
Body-mind theories, 15, 16, 17, 64–65, 67, 69, 70, 71
Brain, 4, 7, 58, 70, 83, 87
British School of Associationism, 19, 52, 80
British School of Empiricism, 14, 53, 79
Buddhism, 1

Causality, 20, 65, 80
Character types, 9, 78

Child care, 43, 93
Child psychology, 31, 40, 51, 53, 88, 89, 92
Clinic, 44, 50, 61
Clinical psychology, 44, 50, 53
Collective unconscious, 49
Color vision, theory of, 28, 56, 81, 82, 85, 87
Common Sense, School of, 19, 53
Comparative psychology, 23, 36, 53, 88, 89
Complex, 47, 48
Conditioning, 12, 38, 53, 90
Confucianism, 1
Consciousness, 10, 15, 16, 24, 30, 33, 34, 43, 46, 67, 69, 75, 79
Contiguity, 8, 20, 42
Cortical localization, 23, 26, 55, 57–58, 83, 86
Courses, first offered, 30, 35, 49, 58
Creative synthesis, 30
Critical Idealism, 20, 52, 65–66, 81

Deduction, 11, 12, 72, 78
Demonic possession, 7, 12
Determinism, 16, 17, 66, 70, 75, 79
Differential psychology, 35, 52, 78, 87
Dissociation, 46, 52, 91
Double-aspect theory, 66, 73
Dualism, 3, 7, 8, 14, 15, 16, 31, 64, 65, 66, 73
Dynamic psychology, 29, 41, 53, 66, 88, 92

Ecology, 52
Educational psychology, 23, 43, 52, 90
Electrical stimulation of the brain, 58, 87
Emanation theory of perception, 5, 6